# Allergies

## Gerald Newman and Eleanor Newman Layfield

Franklin Watts
New York/London/Toronto/Sydney
A Venture Book

Dedication
With love: To Agnes Clune, Jonathan Keith, and
Christopher David, who always wanted to know how
I was doing . . . and to W. David and to Aaron Roy
who both know why I do everything.

Photographs copyright ©: Phototake, Inc.: pp. 10 top (Institut
Pasteur), 10 bottom (Franklin M.D.), 22 (Dennis Kunkel); Photo
Researchers, Inc.: pp. 23 top, 28 bottom, 31 top (all Biophoto
Associates), 46 top (Robert H. Wright), 46 bottom (C.G. Maxwell),
47 (Les Line/National Audubon Society); Lester V. Bergman
Assoc., NY: pp. 23 bottom, 48, 66 top, 74, 81, 88; Mark Sneller:
p. 28 top; American College of Allergy and Immunology; p. 31
bottom; Randy Matusow; pp. 37, 44; The Bettmann Archive:
p. 43; National Jewish Center for Immunology and Respiratory
Medicine: pp. 57, 86 top; Medical Images Inc.: p. 66 bottom
(Nancy Wolfin, M.D.); Peter Arnold Inc.: p. 86 bottom (SIU, School
of Medicine); Custom Medical Stock Photo: p. 89.

Library of Congress Cataloging-in-Publication Data

Newman, Gerald.
   Allergies/Gerald Newman and Eleanor Newman Layfield.
   p.   cm. — (A Venture book)
   Includes bibliographical references and index.
   Summary: Discusses different types of allergies, causes of allergic
reactions, and treatments.
   ISBN 0-531-12516-5
   1.   Allergy—Juvenile literature.   [1. Allergy.]   I. Layfield,
Eleanor Newman.   II. Title.
RC584.N49 1992
616.97—dc20     91-33862 CIP AC

# Contents:

# Allergies

# Introduction:
# What Happened to Cassidy?

Cassidy Jonathan Clune, a curly-haired five-year-old boy, is eagerly waiting for his mom to help him finish dressing for his very first day of school. Neither Cassidy nor his mom can possibly know that within a month of his entering the classroom, he'll not only make new friends, learn to write his name, and finally learn to share, but he'll also be subject to his first *allergy* attack.

In less than one week after starting school, Cassidy caught a cold, not uncommon when a child is first exposed to large groups of other children. Cassidy was exposed to a virus. But because he was in good health, his *immune system*—the defenses produced by the body when a harmful foreign substance enters it—was able to deal with it. And he was back in school four days later. Furthermore, Cassidy's immunological lines of defense produced protection against that virus. So the next time Cassidy's body comes in contact with that virus, his immune system will remember. It will produce large numbers of *antibodies* that will blunt or even block the virus from causing another cold.

One day toward the end of September, Cassidy came home with a runny nose and itchy eyes. He was cranky and passed up his afternoon snack. His mom thought, "Here we go again. Cassidy has another cold." But she was wrong. Cassidy's symptoms didn't disappear after four days. And unlike his previous experience with a cold, Cassidy's sister Jenny didn't catch it, nor did any of his classmates.

After they visited the doctor, Cassidy and his mom found out he had an allergy. Because it was the end of September, the *hay fever* season, it was suspected that *pollen* was causing Cassidy's symptoms. Once it was determined what Cassidy was allergic to, the doctor could prescribe medications to alleviate Cassidy's discomfort until the hay fever season was over.

As far as Cassidy was concerned, his problems were solved. Once again he was enjoying school. But his mom had questions. She wanted to know what caused Cassidy's allergy. She told the doctor, "No one in our family has an allergy." She asked, "What happened with Cassidy? Will it happen again? Will he grow out of it?" Although she had heard of allergies and had some friends who suffered from them, she had never experienced the syndrome so close to home. Now she wanted to know everything.

# Chemistry of an Allergic Reaction

In Cassidy's case, an *allergen*, a trigger to an allergic reaction, entered Cassidy's nose. However, this was not the first time this specific allergen entered Cassidy's nose. For an allergic reaction to take place, the body must first be *sensitized, or exposed,* to the allergen. In Cassidy's case, the allergen was pollen. Cassidy's immune system, already sensitized to the pollen, began to defend Cassidy against it.

First, blood cells called *macrophages* determine what the intruder is. The macrophages report this information to *lymphocytes*, which are white blood cells, the front-line fighters of the immune system.

The lymphocytes produce antibodies to get rid of the pollen grains. So far, so good. During this phase, Cassidy felt no symptoms. His immune system worked just as it had in the early stages of the cold he had at the beginning of the school term. But that's where the similarity ends.

The antibodies produced by the lymphocytes to defend against the allergen are of a special type. They

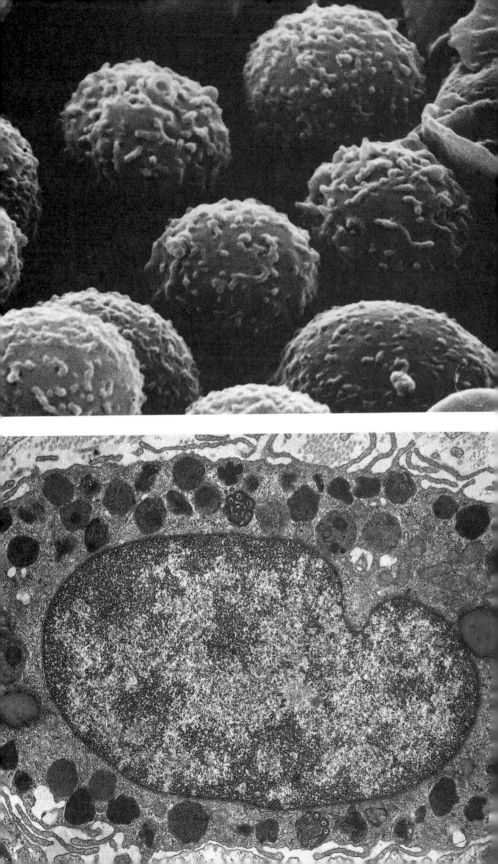

are called *IgE immunoglobulins.* In a person who has no allergies, like Cassidy's sister Jenny, very low levels of IgE immunoglobulins are produced in the bloodstream when an allergen enters it. But for Cassidy, it is different. When an allergen enters Cassidy's bloodstream, his lymphocytes produce many IgE immunoglobulin antibodies. As the antibodies increase, they attach themselves to the surfaces of *basophil* cells, which are also white blood cells, and to *mast cells*, which are located in body tissues.

Once the antibodies are attached, the basophil and mast cells become sensitized to the pollen grains and become the site of an allergic response. If we look more closely at the basophil and mast cells, we'll see that they are filled with granules. The granules are enclosed by a membrane that prevents the chemical compounds inside from being released into the rest of the cells. These chemicals are known as *mediators*. One of the mediators, called *histamine*, is the culprit causing Cassidy's allergic symptoms.

So what finally happened to Cassidy as the pollen grains entered his nose? His immune system worked, but it worked to produce symptoms instead of blocking them. Cassidy's body produced loads of IgE immunoglobulin antibodies, which then attached to basophil and mast cells. In some way that has not been discovered by researchers, the membranes surrounding

(Top) High-magnification view of lymphocytes (white blood cells). Lymphocytes produce antibodies.
(Bottom) Cross-sectional view of a mast cell. The dark areas surrounding the cell are newly released histamine.

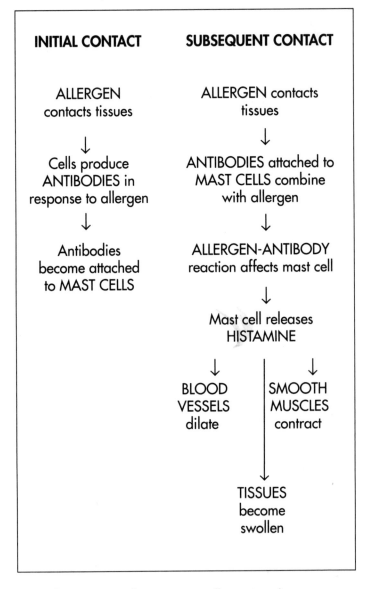

**INITIAL CONTACT**

ALLERGEN
contacts tissues

↓

Cells produce
ANTIBODIES in
response to allergen

↓

Antibodies
become attached
to MAST CELLS

**SUBSEQUENT CONTACT**

ALLERGEN contacts
tissues

↓

ANTIBODIES attached to
MAST CELLS combine
with allergen

↓

ALLERGEN-ANTIBODY
reaction affects mast cell

↓

Mast cell releases
HISTAMINE

↓                    ↓

BLOOD              SMOOTH
VESSELS            MUSCLES
dilate             contract

↓

TISSUES
become
swollen

The sequence of events in an allergy. Initial contact
sensitizes the body to the allergen by stimulating the
production of antibodies. Subsequent exposure to the
allergen may trigger a physical reaction.

the granules inside those cells broke down, and histamine was released. The histamine seeped into surrounding tissues and blood vessels. Histamine causes increased secretions in the eyes and nose, and can cause any part of the body to become swollen with fluid. Cassidy's nose soon began to run and his eyes started to itch.[1]

Depending on where the chemical mediators are released in the body, different symptoms occur. For instance, in Cassidy's lungs, the mediators can narrow breathing passages and perhaps cause an *asthma* attack. Cassidy has already shown what happens when mediators travel to the nose and eyes: tissues swell, causing a stuffed nose, and eyes itch because histamine is in the blood vessels surrounding the eyes.

If histamine travels to the blood vessels in the head, a headache or sinusitis (an inflammation of the sinus cavities) can result. Traveling to the intestinal lining, mediators can cause stomach cramps or diarrhea. The more mediators released, the more severe the reaction will be. In any case, the person who suffers an allergic reaction will generally be miserable.[2]

For the sufferer it's less important to know how an allergic reaction occurs than to know what kind of relief is available. Sometimes that relief comes in the form of an over-the-counter, or nonprescription, medicine containing an *antihistamine,* which reacts with histamine that has already been produced by the body and stops it from reacting with body tissues.

But for researchers who are studying better ways to treat the symptoms of an allergy or prevent the reaction from happening altogether, learning how an allergy occurs in the cells is of primary importance.

# The Human Factor

It is estimated that from 30 million to 40 million people in the United States suffer from allergies. Increases in that figure can be related to increases in chemicals in the air, to new substances or agents such as those added to foods to preserve them, and even to the creation of new medicines.

While there is a strong genetic tendency toward allergies, *specific* sensitivities are not inherited. It is the *potential* to develop an allergy that is passed on from parent to child and not necessarily to every child in the family. It is generally agreed that if one parent has an allergy, there is a 30 percent chance that his or her child will have a greater potential to develop an allergy. If both parents have allergies, the risk doubles, increasing to 60 percent.

Researchers still do not know why one child develops allergies while others in the family do not. Furthermore, it is not understood why a parent may be allergic to a specific substance and the child may not be allergic to that substance. When it was determined that Cassidy had an allergic reaction to pollen, everyone in his family was tested. Cassidy's mother was found to be allergy-prone but only to cats and dogs. And whereas Cassidy's allergic reaction was intense, his mother's reaction to cats and dogs was relatively mild. That may have accounted for her earlier belief that no one in her family had an allergy. So intensity of reaction is not inherited either.

Allergies may develop at any age but are more likely to appear first in childhood than during the adult years. Many scientists theorize that this may be because of the greater sensitivity of the child's immune system. However, it is not uncommon for adults to develop allergies when they have never had an allergic attack before. There are many cases of adults who develop hay fever, for instance, apparently out of the blue. But that is not the case. A person can, in fact, carry around a potential sensitivity to a particular allergen for many years. Then one day, for reasons that still puzzle researchers, the potential becomes an actuality, and the adult sneezes and wheezes as if he or she had had that allergy since childhood. Indeed, one of the authors of this book can confirm that fact from her own experience.

A frequently heard bit of misinformation is that a child who develops an allergy will "grow out of it." Although it is true that the immune system becomes less sensitive as we mature, a person remains allergic, though perhaps to a lesser degree. Additionally, a young child may react poorly to some of the more uncomfortable symptoms of a particular allergy. For instance, some symptoms of asthma can be very frightening to a youngster. But as the child grows more mature in behavior, an allergic attack is handled far better.

During the adolescent years, when the body is experiencing hormonal upheavals, it may appear as if the allergies have disappeared, as is frequently observed with asthma. However, when the adolescent grows to adulthood, it is likely that the allergic attacks may reappear. According to the most recent tracking statistics, about one-third of the young adults who suffered allergies as children may find that the allergic attacks have disappeared. But the remaining two-thirds will continue to have symptoms. Some will suffer more frequent attacks and even worse symptoms than they had as children.

Therefore, it is safe to say that no general statement can be made about the ability of a child to "outgrow" a particular allergy. Even though the statement may offer hope to a youngster who suffers a great deal, the odds are that the only thing he or she may outgrow is a negative attitude toward the allergy.

# Symptoms of Allergic Diseases

We know that allergens, such as the grains of pollen that entered young Cassidy's nose, trigger allergic episodes. Allergens include a wide range of substances, from apples to zucchini, from airedales to zebras. The most common allergens are pollens from trees, grasses, and weeds. Molds, dust, foods, industrial pollutants, animal dander, insect stings, and household chemicals, such as detergent or perfume, are also allergens.

Allergens are classified by the way in which they enter the human body:

- Ingestants are the substances we eat.
- Contactants are materials we touch.
- Injected materials are chemicals or medicines injected into our bodies.
- Inhalants are airborne substances that we inhale, or breathe in.

The chart below shows the types of allergens responsible for the symptoms of allergic diseases. One allergen

## COMMON SYMPTOMS OF ALLERGIC DISEASES

| Affected Organ | Type of Symptom | Possible Allergen | Allergic Disease |
|---|---|---|---|
| The skin | Sores | Contactant Injectant | Dermatitis, eczema |
| | Wheals | Ingestant Contactant Injectant | Hives |
| | Intense itch | Contactant Ingestant Injectant | Dermatitis, eczema, hives |
| Upper respiratory tract | Runny nose, itchy throat and eyes, sneezing | Inhalant | Allergic rhinitis |
| Lower respiratory tract | Cough, thick mucus, wheezing, shortness of breath | Inhalant Ingestant Injectant | Asthma |
| Gastro-intestinal tract | Stomachache, colic, constipation, diarrhea | Ingestant Injectant | Food allergy |
| Ears | Itch or ache | Inhalant | Allergic rhinitis |
| Eyes | Itching, tearing, burning, swelling | Inhalant Contactant Ingestant Injectant | Allergic rhinitis Conjunctivitis Food allergy Insect sting |
| Mouth | Swelling of mucous tissue | Ingestant Injectant | Food allergy Insect sting/bite |

can cause different symptoms in different organs of the body. For instance, pollen triggering an allergic episode can cause itchy eyes and throat or sneezing and runny nose. When those symptoms present themselves, the condition may be the allergic disease hay fever.

However, sneezing does not necessarily indicate hay fever. The person sneezing may have a cold. It will take careful observation to determine the difference between a cold and hay fever. For instance, Cassidy's initial sneezes were due to a cold caused by a virus. When Cassidy came home sneezing a few weeks later, his mom thought he had a cold again. But as the symptoms persisted, even after a visit to Cassidy's doctor, it was clear that something other than a virus was causing Cassidy's discomfort. And that's when Cassidy's mother and doctor agreed there was a possibility that Cassidy might have an allergy.

The chart below also classifies the common symptoms of allergic diseases by the organ of the body subject to the symptoms.

This chart categorizes only a few of the symptoms of the most common allergic diseases. But doctors who want to provide the best possible treatment for their patients must also determine specifically what is causing or triggering the symptoms. That's when an in-depth knowledge of allergens is most important.

# Inhalant Allergens

Inhalants (airborne substances we inhale) are the most common cause of allergic reactions. They not only cause respiratory symptoms, but they can worsen other complaints such as eczema and gastrointestinal difficulties.

Heading the list of inhalant allergens is pollen, followed by molds, dust, animal dander, smoke, and chemical pollutants. Other airborne particles that can be considered culprits include insect parts, soaps, detergents, certain chemicals, and household cleaning agents. Although allergic attacks from soaps and certain chemicals are less frequently noted than attacks from pollen, those who have allergic reactions to these chemical inhalants suffer just as much as a person who is allergic to pollen.

## PLANT POLLENS

Plants emit pollen as part of their reproductive cycle. Pollen particles are small, egg-shaped male germ cells necessary for fertilization, with the average particle being smaller than the width of a human hair. Pollen enters the respiratory passages (nose and mouth) and triggers the symptoms of hay fever. Surprisingly, the pollen that is carried from flower to flower is not an important factor in triggering hay fever. That kind of pollen is too sticky and heavy to be airborne in large amounts.

The pollens of such trees as elm, birch, ash, hickory, poplar, sycamore, maple, cypress, and walnut are often the cause of early spring *allergic rhinitis*.

Late-spring and early-summer allergic rhinitis is caused by pollinating *grasses*, such as timothy, bermuda, orchard, sweet vernal, red top, and some blue grasses.[1] Ragweed pollen is considered to be the major cause of hay fever in North America, but other weeds whose pollen can cause hay fever are: sagebrush, pigweed, tumbleweed, Russian thistle, and cockleweed.

Not all plants emit allergy-producing pollens. In fact, until recently, it was thought that goldenrod, a plant that appears in the late summer and early fall in the eastern and midwestern United States, was a primary source of allergy-producing pollen. Further research revealed that it was the ragweed, a plant that appears at exactly the same time and area as the goldenrod, that was the cause.

### Weather Influences

Each plant has a period of pollination that remains consistent from year to year. However, the weather can affect the amount of pollen in the air at any time. It has been determined that monitoring the weather just before a hay fever season can provide a fairly accurate indication of what to expect. For instance, a mild winter followed by an early spring provides the perfect environment for an increase in pollen reproduction and can result in a pollen "invasion" in June. If there is such an "invasion," it would follow that ragweed and other

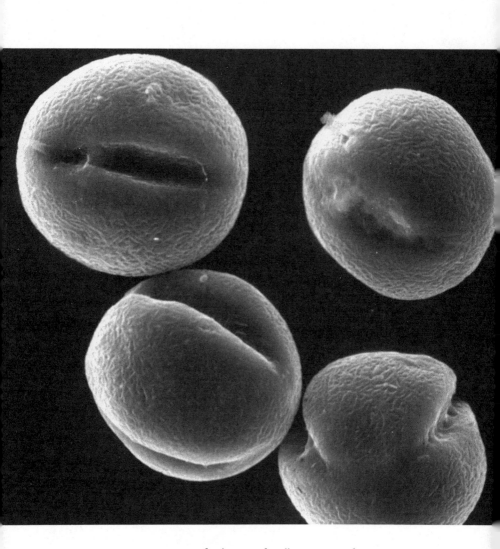

Magnified view of pollen grains of
maple-tree flowers, which can cause
allergic rhinitis in the early spring.
(Facing page, top) Magnified view of the flower
of the ragweed. Note the spherical
pollen grains. They are a leading
cause of hay fever in summer and fall.
(Bottom) Higher-magnification view
of ragweed pollen

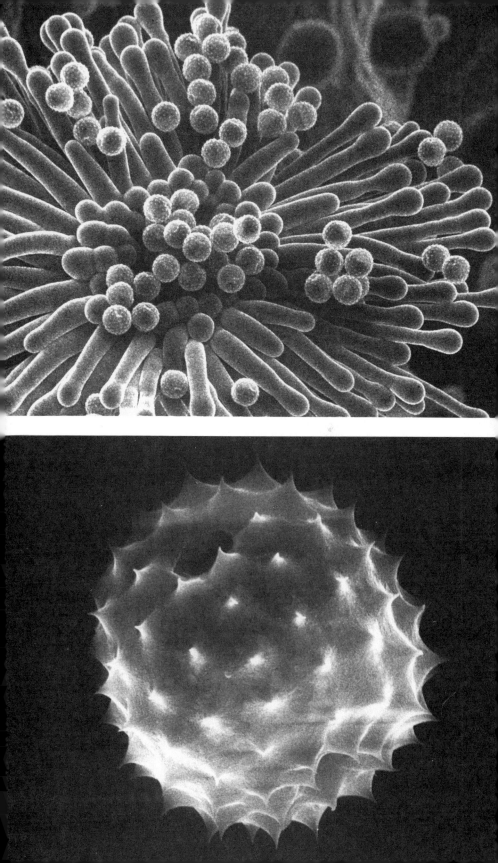

weed pollens will reproduce at higher levels and produce a "bumper crop," peaking in mid-August or early September, according to Dr. Sidney Friedlander, a clinical professor of medicine at the University of Florida.

Armed with this information, a hay fever sufferer can visit his or her doctor and prepare in advance as strong a defense as possible, through a series of allergy shots, diet, and exercise.

### Location Influences

In addition to the weather, location determines when a hay fever season begins and what kinds of plants will emit allergy-producing pollens. The chart on page 26 takes into consideration both variables of preceding weather and location to forecast a typical hay fever season in various regions of the United States. The chart also indicates some of the varieties of plants for each region that are known to produce the pollen causing hay fever.[2]

This chart can be particularly helpful for the allergy-prone person who must travel nationwide on a regular basis. From the information provided it can be concluded that our nationwide traveler would be wise to stay clear of the Southeast from July through December, with the exception of Florida's southern tip, which is nearly free of ragweed. The western states offer some relief because the area produces less pollen than most of the rest of country; the land and altitude do not provide the best growing conditions for plants emitting allergy-producing pollen.

As a general rule of thumb: the farther north you go, the later the pollinating season and therefore the later the hay fever season.

Trees pollinate earliest, from February or March to April or May, depending on the location. For instance, in the northern United States trees start pollinating in April, while in the South, trees pollinate as early as January. Grasses follow next in the pollination cycle, beginning in May and continuing until mid-July. Weeds usually pollinate in late summer.

## Lost Arizona

During the late 1950s and through the 1960s, Arizona, a state in the southwest region of the United States, was considered a mecca for allergy sufferers. But unfortunately, Arizona is no longer free from pollen and ragweed invasions. Ironically, the very attractiveness of Arizona induced thousands of Americans to move there. And with the increases in population came new construction, new industries, and more housing to support the population. As new communities were developed, so did their landscapes. Trees and grasses were planted in profusion. By the late 1970s, Arizona was no longer considered a safe haven for allergy sufferers. In fact, Tucson, Arizona, citizens face a potential fine of $300 a day if lawns are not closely cropped. The city also bans the sale of mulberry and olive trees, because they produce great amounts of pollen.[3]

Things are so bad in Tucson that nearly one-half of its residents suffer from asthma or hay fever, four times the national average. In addition to ordinances to help combat pollen and mold, the county health department created the Office of Pollen and Mold Control. Heading that office is Mark Sneller, a microbiologist, who gathers data every morning from numerous pollen and mold monitors located throughout the city and reports his findings to the newspapers and broadcast media. For the residents of Tucson, that's front-page news.

For the rest of his day Dr. Sneller will answer phone calls from residents and monitor areas of the city where there may be problems. For instance, at one school the children and teachers were suffering hay fever attacks. Inspectors checked the air ducts and cooling systems to make sure they were clean, and when

## A REGIONAL FORECAST FOR HAY FEVER

| Section of U.S. | Weather Preceding Season | Forecast |
| --- | --- | --- |
| Northeast | Mild winter | Major allergy problems through June, ragweed and mold spores will hit mid-August through October |
| Southeast | Winter freeze | Ragweed season extended from July to December. |
| Midwest | Mild winter, warm spring | Rapid growth of ragweed, lamb's quarters, and Russian thistle will produce severe allergy symptoms |
| Southwest | Normal winter/spring | Moderate symptoms through July, high ragweed levels August through September |
| Rockies | Mild winter, warm spring | Low-level grass pollen through July, heavier levels of ragweed, sagebrush, and Russian thistle pollen July through late August |
| West | Normal winter/spring | Pollens from English plantain and yellow dock cause usual allergy problems in June and July |

that was done, they called Dr. Sneller. Through careful observation, Dr. Sneller noted that the symptoms were worse among teachers and students whose classrooms were close to a back door of the school. Teachers had frequently left the door opened to let in the "fresh air." What Dr. Sneller saw that everyone else had not taken into consideration was that the back doors opened onto a grassy playing field. In addition, the doors faced south, directly in the line of the prevailing winds. Dr. Sneller monitored the rooms and noted that when the wind blew, it carried the allergenic grass pollen from the grass directly into the classrooms, where it would increase to high concentrations. Once Dr. Sneller persuaded the teachers to keep the back door closed, the symptoms gradually lessened.

Dr. Sneller also travels around the nation helping to set up offices in communities that have the same problems as Tucson.[4]

## MOLDS AND FUNGI

*Spores* released from molds and *fungi* can cause a chronic runny nose or even asthma. Fungi and molds thrive in warm, moist conditions. They occur both inside and outside the home. Some indoor sources of mold and fungi are:

- Damp basement and crawl spaces
- Bathrooms and showers
- Window frames
- Utility rooms
- Houseplants
- Rubber and foam pillows
- Stuffed animals
- Furniture
- Mattresses

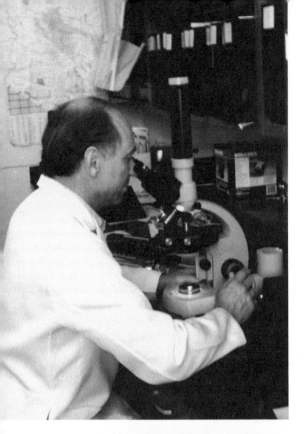

(Left) Mark Sneller is a microbiologist at the Office of Pollen and Mold Detection in Tuscon, Arizona. In the postwar years, when migrants from wetter climes came to Arizona, they all too often brought a taste for their favorite plants with them. Residents with pollen allergies suffered as a result. (Below) Spores of the rhizopus bread mold. Mold spores are a leading cause of allergic symptoms.

Air conditioning equipment, vaporizers, and dehumidifiers provide relief for many allergy sufferers, but if the machines are not kept clean, mold will collect in them and cause allergy symptoms. Some examples of indoor mold are aspergillus, mucor, rhizopus, and the more familiar penicillium, which can be easily detected on breads and cheeses. All of these molds can cause symptoms all year round in sensitive individuals.

Another story about Dr. Sneller illustrates how important it is to keep homes free of mold. He was asked to visit a home in which a young boy, very much like Cassidy, continued to suffer from allergy symptoms, even though the home was free of pets, plants, carpets, and other allergens. Dr. Sneller had to agree that at first glance the home was allergy-free. After a room-to-room search, Dr. Sneller found himself in the kitchen. He said to the mother, "Well, I guess we can rule out the kitchen as long as the refrigerator has been cleaned underneath."[5] The fact was that the refrigerator had never been moved. Sneller moved the refrigerator and showed how water and heat provide a perfect environment for mold to grow. He also pointed out how the refrigerator motor pushes the air filled with mold spores into the house. The boy's mother immediately cleaned the floor underneath the refrigerator and the surrounding area. After another visit Dr. Sneller found that the young boy's symptoms had diminished a great deal.

Outdoors, mold and fungi can be found on leaf and plant surfaces and on decomposing plant materials. They may be present at all times during the year, except when snow is on the ground. The spores of molds and fungi are easily spread by the wind.

Around the United States, molds and fungi are most prevalent in the Midwest, where they grow on grains such as corn, wheat, oats, and barley. The eastern part of the United States is also affected because mold can grow on grass, dead leaves, and other vegetation in this area. April through November is the usual season for molds and fungi to grow rapidly.

The most common examples of molds are *Alternaria* and *Cladosporium*, which are responsible for the majority of allergic reactions. They thrive in Nebraska, Kansas, Indiana, Wisconsin, Ohio, Michigan, Iowa, and Missouri and are also found to a lesser degree in the southern, eastern, and Rocky Mountain areas. However, there is a decrease in the number of molds and fungi in high-altitude areas and in very dry regions such as southwestern California.[6]

## DUST

Dust is all around us and is a major source of discomfort for allergy sufferers. In fact, 10 to 15 percent of the population and 40 percent of those who have asthma or multiple allergies suffer year round from allergy to dust.

Unfortunately, there is no way to keep a home dust-free, even if the people who reside there are perfectionists. Dust is not composed of dirt or soil but is the result of a combination of breakdown products of organic materials such as animal dander, wool and linen fibers, feathers, and plant residue.

One of the inhabitants of dust is an almost microscopic eight-legged creature called the house *dust*

(Top) House dust magnified 575X. Small fibers can be seen. Can you make out pollen grains? (Bottom) The dust mite is found in almost all households. Its excrement can be a potent allergen.

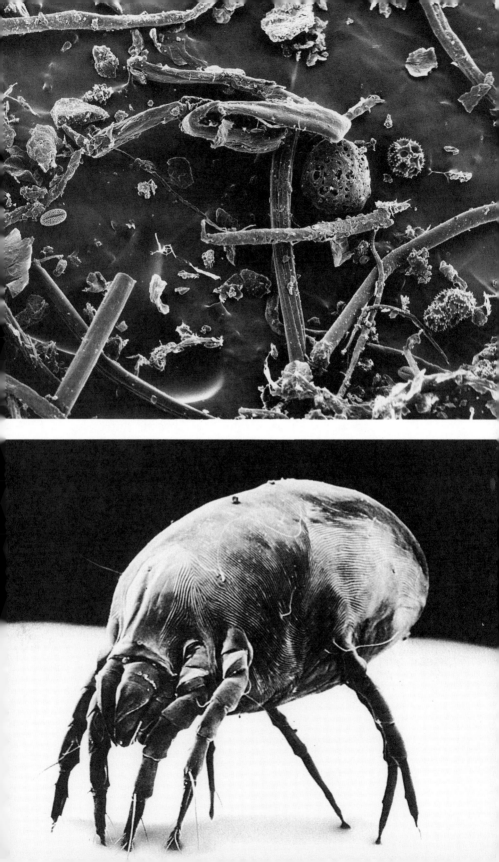

*mite*. But it is not the mite itself to which allergy-prone people are sensitive. It is the tiny, tough pellet of fecal matter that the dust mite excretes after it has eaten a meal of flakes of skin from people or pets.

Dust mites thrive when the temperature and humidity are in the seventies. In the winter, dust mites continue to survive because it is now so common to seal windows and insulate homes with carpeting in order to conserve energy. The increased insulation keeps the temperature and humidity high enough for the dust mite to thrive.

Dust mites are so small, it is estimated that seven thousand of them could fit on a dime. They are generally found in areas where one finds skin flakes: bedding, upholstered furniture, and carpets. In fact, fussy homemakers can cause more of a problem by vacuuming a carpet or remaking a bed because the pellets of a dust mite can become airborne long enough for people to inhale them.

Both in the United States and abroad, studies on dust mites and their relationship to asthma reveal that children who were heavily exposed to dust mites during infancy were much more likely to have asthma by the age of eleven. Additionally, it was shown that among asthmatic children who had a sensitivity to dust mites, reduction of the mites in their bedrooms to close to zero led to dramatic improvement in the asthma symptoms.[7]

## ANIMAL DANDER

Animal dander is dried dead skin cells (from any animal) or dried saliva (from cats). It can be the cause of chronic hay fever symptoms in people who are allergy-prone, especially children.

Not only are cats and dogs included in the category of animals to which people have a sensitivity, but horses, rabbits, hamsters, mice, rats, and birds are known to cause hay fever symptoms.

Even the dishes used by animals for their food and water can cause problems. It has been shown that if the dishes are not kept absolutely clean, molds and fungi develop, and their airborne spores can cause allergic reactions.

Birds have always been common animal pets, and most recently, exotic birds have become extremely popular. However, dried bird droppings that are dispersed in the air are known to cause serious lung disorders.

Not even fish are considered safe because the water in which they live may house mold and fungi spores if the tanks are not cleaned on a regular basis. The filters used in fish tanks must also be cleaned regularly, because the enclosed moist area is a better environment for molds and fungi than the water tank itself.

The best an allergy-prone person can do to avoid the symptoms of hay fever, asthma, and other respiratory complaints is to stay as far away as possible from animals.[8]

## SMOKE

Smoke is not classified as an allergen. But as an irritant, smoke may cause asthmatic symptoms, such as *wheezing* and shortness of breath. Allergy-prone people who are exposed to tobacco smoke or the smoke from wood-burning stoves and fireplaces, candles, and incense, especially in closed-in areas, will experience asthmatic symptoms almost immediately. The symptoms disappear when the person leaves the area in which the offensive smoke is found.

## POLLUTANTS

No place in the United States is entirely free from air pollution, whether from automobile or industrial emissions. We are all affected when the air is heavily polluted, but those who are allergy-prone—especially those who suffer from asthma—may find their outdoor activities curtailed when there is a pollution alert.

Indoors, chemical pollutants from household detergents, soaps, and cleaning fluids can trigger hay fever symptoms and other respiratory problems. Most airborne chemical pollutants that trigger coughing, sneezing, and tearing eyes have a pungent odor. One example is ammonia, which is found in many household cleaners. Ammonia is an excellent cleaner, but a person who is particularly sensitive would do well to use some of the newer detergents and cleansers that are considered nontoxic.

# Ingestant Allergens

When Cassidy Jonathan Clune was born, his pediatrician suggested that milk not be included in Cassidy's diet. The pediatrician was concerned that Cassidy might develop colic, a condition found among newborn babies that causes them to be cranky, sleepless, and generally fretful. Cassidy's doctor made this suggestion when he learned that Cassidy's father thought he might have been allergic to milk and milk products when he was a baby. And the doctor did not want to take chances.

Surprisingly, the idea that food allergies could be a recognized medical problem did not occur to the medical profession until the mid-1940s.

Hippocrates, an early Greek physician and philosopher, was the first to note that cow's milk could cause health problems for some people. But he had no science to determine what part of the cow's milk was causing a problem, nor did he know about the concept of allergy as we know it today.

So if Cassidy's doctor seemed to be overly cautious by eliminating milk from Cassidy's diet, it was because

Cassidy's father was born during the time when food allergy was first beginning to be recognized.

The U.S. Department of Agriculture estimates that about 34 million adults and children are allergic to some food products. However, many adverse reactions to food are not truly allergic reactions. They are presumed to be allergies only because no other cause can be found, and once the offending food is removed from the diet, the symptoms disappear. An allergy diagnosis depends on the presence of *IgE antibodies* in the blood.

Food allergens, those parts of food that cause allergic reactions, are usually proteins. Most can cause reactions even after they have been cooked or mixed with the chemicals of digestion.

Many food products have been studied to establish allergen content. Recent studies in the United States show that cow's milk, eggs, peanuts, wheat, and soy are the most common food allergens. Shrimp, codfish, and crab also have been identified as food allergens.

Virtually any food or drink can trigger an adverse reaction in a susceptible person. Symptoms of a true allergic reaction or one that mimics it (no IgE antibodies found in the blood) may appear. In any case, the symptoms can take any of the various forms that characterize allergies: wheezing and shortness of breath, hives, eczema, hay fever, colic, diarrhea and vomiting, and chronic stomachache.

A severe allergic reaction to food is called *anaphylaxis* and can sometimes be fatal. Foods frequently listed as causing anaphylaxis in susceptible people include peanuts, nuts, shellfish, eggs, and seeds. Foods

(Top) Milk and milk products are common food allergens.
(Bottom) Many people are allergic to foods made from wheat.

such as milk, chocolate, barley, citrus fruits, melons, bananas, tomatoes, spinach, corn, potatoes, and soybeans also have been known to cause anaphylaxis, though reactions occur less frequently.[1]

One person who suffers severe allergic reactions to a particular food is Richard Burke, who resides in New York City and is allergic to any and all forms of fowl, not one of the better-known food allergens.[2] When he eats out, Mr. Burke has to make sure that no fowl, such as chicken, duck, or turkey, is on his plate. He also must make sure that chicken stock is not used in the preparation of any food, such as gravies or soups. On several occasions, when he was assured that his food was free from fowl of any kind, Mr. Burke suffered headache, nausea, and dizziness within a few seconds of ingesting the food. Sometimes, the reactions become so severe that Mr. Burke must seek emergency medical treatment. Although Mr. Burke's syndrome is unusual, in the case of food allergy it is wise to be extremely cautious in preparing food to avoid the possibility of a serious reaction.

## FOOD ADDITIVES

To keep foods from perishing on the shelf, to retain or enhance food color, and to improve the flavor of certain foods, chemicals called food additives are used. Although the additives serve a useful purpose, they may cause allergic symptoms in susceptible people.

Monosodium glutamate is a taste enhancer used in processed peanuts, dried tomatoes, soups, Asian foods, and soy sauce. It is even sold by itself to be used in punching up the flavor of foods that are prepared at home. Monosodium glutamate has been known to cause distress in sensitive people. Common complaints are dizziness, headaches, and body aches immediately after the food containing MSG has been ingested. The person appears to be suffering from the early stages of flu or a cold, but the symptoms disappear after a few hours. Those who especially enjoy dining on Asian dishes now have the option of advising the chef whether or not to prepare food with monosodium glutamate.

Sulfites are used to preserve food and sanitize containers for fermented beverages such as wine. Sulfiting agents such as sulfur dioxide, sodium, and potassium sulfite are found in canned, frozen, and dehydrated foods. Dried fruit, processed grain foods (including cookies and crackers), shrimp, beer, wine coolers, and cider contain sulfites.

Five to 10 percent of the people who suffer from asthma are sensitive to sulfites. As little as 1 milligram of a sulfiting agent can cause an asthma attack. In addition, sulfiting agents can cause reactions such as chest tightness, hives, abdominal cramps, diarrhea, lowered blood pressure, lightheadedness, weakness, and an elevated pulse rate.

## FOOD DYES

The Food, Drug, and Cosmetic Act of 1938 initiated the labeling of certain food and beverage dyes with the term "FD&C." The dyes are additionally identified by color and number. When looking at the labels of certain foods, you will see "FD&C yellow No. 5" or "FD&C red No. 3." These dyes are added to foods to make them look better, and they usually cannot be identified by taste.

FD&C yellow No. 5, or tartrazine, is the food dye that has been studied the longest. Tartrazine is found in tacos, potato chips, some medicine capsules, some toothpastes, and many other products. It has been found that tartrazine may cause hives. People who are sensitive to tartrazine may also be sensitive to aspirin.

It is most important that those who are found to be sensitive to food additives carefully read the labels of all packaged foods to make sure the foods are safe for them to eat. The Food and Drug Administration (FDA) enacted a law in the early 1970s that all packaged and processed foods carry a list of their ingredients. It's not only a good idea to check the labels if you have a sensitivity to food additives; it's also worthwhile to check labels if you want to avoid sugars or salt or are on a special diet.[3]

The diagnosis of a food allergy is often time-consuming. The proliferation of more processed foods and new ways to prepare them can add to the confusion. But with careful, patient sleuthing, the food offender can be detected through a process called the food *elimination test*. This test is conducted by a physician working closely with the patient. A diary is kept of a patient's food intake over a period of time. Foods that are suspected of causing an allergic reaction are introduced one at a time. If there is no reaction, that food can be eliminated from the list of suspected allergens. The process continues until a reaction occurs. The test is not considered complete until all of the suspected allergens are introduced and then eliminated from or added to the list of known food allergens for the particular patient. Once the offending foods are known, diets can be developed that avoid the chance of ingesting those food or food additives that cause the allergic symptoms.

# Injectant and Contactant Allergens

## INJECTANTS

An injectant is a substance that is injected into the body. If the injectant results in rashes, swelling, or breathing difficulties, it is an allergen. Injectants can be classified as (1) drugs or medicine and (2) insect stings or bites.

### Insect Stings

The venom from the sting of an insect is called an injectant. The common stinging insects—the honeybee, the hornet, the wasp, and the yellow jacket—belong to the same biological family, Hymenoptera.[1]

Stings from these insects usually produce localized symptoms, such as a welt or a small swelling. This is not considered an allergic reaction. It is a normal reaction to the toxic substances contained in the insect venom. An allergic reaction occurs when a sting that occurs on one area of the body causes problems in other areas. For instance, if someone were stung on the arm and, in addition, had difficulty breathing or developed a rash across his or her chest, that person would be suffering an allergic reaction to an insect sting.

As in all allergic reactions, no one can be allergic to an insect sting unless he or she was stung previously. That person's immune system will then be sensitized to the particular insect's venom and will develop an allergic reaction the next time a stinging incident occurs.

The severity of the allergic symptoms can range from a mild outbreak of hives to a severe reaction such as *anaphylaxis*, which is characterized by a sudden drop in blood pressure, generalized swelling, and difficulty in breathing. The more times a person is stung by an insect to which he or she is allergic, the greater the chance of anaphylaxis. Allergic reactions can appear within minutes of the sting, or sometimes the reaction may occur hours later.

In recent years the sting of the fire ant, which is currently found in southern parts of the United States around the Gulf area, has resulted in allergic symptoms. The fire ant is a member of the same insect family as bees, wasps, hornets, and yellow jackets. The insect bites and then stings. Within twenty-four hours a blister-like eruption appears. The allergic symptoms that occur can be as mild as skin itching and hives and as serious as anaphylactic shock.

### Drugs

Drugs can be ingested, come in contact with the skin, and be injected. According to the FDA (the Food and Drug Administration) there were about forty thousand adverse drug reactions in 1989.

An adverse drug reaction can be described as a response to a drug that results in unwanted, uncomfortable, and unpleasant symptoms.

However, those symptoms do not always indicate a true allergy. They may occur for a number of reasons,

Fire ants feeding on an unopened flower bud of okra,
in a photo taken in Mobile County, Alabama.
People sensitive to its sting can suffer severe
allergic reactions.

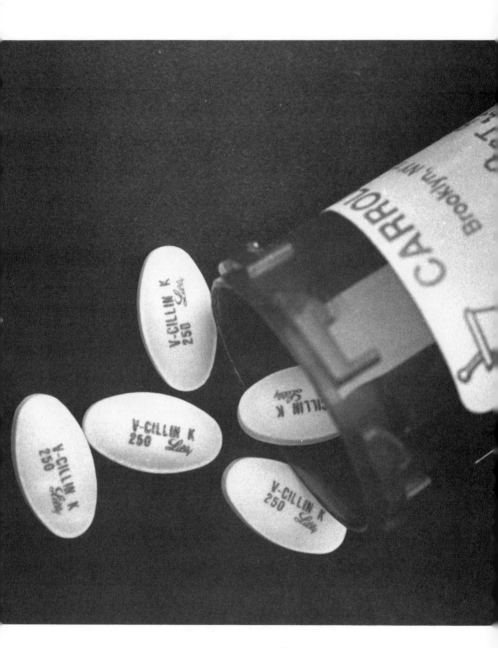

Many people develop allergic reactions
to certain pharmaceuticals.

such as intolerance, unusual reactions, overdose, side effects, drug interactions, and psychological responses.

Very few people show a true allergic reaction to drugs. As was noted previously, the only sure detector of an allergic response is the presence of IgE antibodies in the blood. Many drugs may prove to be allergens, but so far medical science has not developed a test sophisticated enough to demonstrate the presence of IgE antibodies to drugs. An exception is the drug penicillin, which is considered an allergen because it can be tested for.[2]

The symptoms exhibited during an allergic reaction to penicillin can range from the inconvenience of an itchy, measles-like rash to the life-threatening symptoms of anaphylactic shock. In any event, once it is determined that a person is allergic to penicillin, it is important that medical personnel are made aware of this tendency. Hives and rashes are uncomfortable, but anaphylactic shock can cause death in a very short time. When there is a question about whether a person is sensitive to penicillin, the safest course of treatment is not to administer the penicillin.

Aspirin is widely used across the United States. In fact, over 30 million pounds were consumed (ingested or injected) last year. Because it is used so universally, aspirin is second only to penicillin as a cause of adverse drug reactions. However, a reaction to aspirin is not a true allergy. In medical terms, the reaction is known as an *idiosyncrasy*. It means that there is an abnormal response to a drug, although no definitive allergic response patterns can be found. The most common symptoms of aspirin sensitivity are hives. Additionally, there is a condition known as *aspirin triad*, which consists of severe bronchial asthma, sinusitis, and nasal polyps. People who suffer from these symptoms, most of whom are adults, should not use aspirin. Fortunately, for those who are sensitive to aspirin, substitutes

Learn to identify these three poisonous plants:
poison ivy (facing page, above);
poison oak (facing page, below);
poison sumac (above). It could save you
considerable grief the next time you
venture into a wooded area.

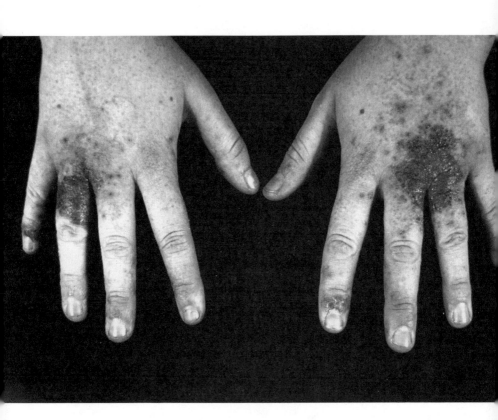

This rash resulted from
wearing rings that
contain nickel.

such as acetaminophen are available. Two popular
brands are Tylenol and Datril.

Some people are sensitive to local anesthetics or
painkillers. One of the most frequently used is
Xylocaine, which can be injected or used topically in
the form of ointments, or creams. Reactions to
Xylocaine can range from mild discomfort to rashes to
a life-and-death situation and can be classified as toxic,
psychological, or allergic.

Allergic reactions to injected painkillers are extremely rare. Usually, an allergic reaction occurs when a person uses a cream or ointment containing a painkiller such as Xylocaine and develops a contact sensitivity such as a rash or an itch.

Toxic reactions are more frequent. They usually occur when an injection is administered poorly and enters a blood vessel or when the drug is absorbed too quickly.

A psychological response can happen to anyone. For some, the mere idea of going to the dentist or receiving an injection can initiate rapid heartbeat, dizziness, or fainting.

Insulin, the drug used to control the disease diabetes, can produce allergy-like responses, from local skin eruption to generalized shock.

If a person is truly allergic to a drug and does not exhibit a toxic or psychological reaction, chances are the allergy to that drug will last. Since there are still no accurate tests to determine drug sensitivity in advance, it is best to be cautious when taking new drugs. Giving the physician the details of previous responses to certain drugs will be helpful. Also, discussing the normal side effects of a new drug will help in reducing the anxiety some patients might have because of previous adverse drug reactions.

## CONTACTANTS

A contactant is a substance or material, including some plants, that causes eruptions when it comes in direct contact with the skin.

A contact sensitivity is caused only by substances that touch the body (external substances). Contact sensitivities occur in three main forms: allergic *contact dermatitis*, irritant contact dermatitis, and photoallergic contact dermatitis.

For the purposes of this chapter, we will focus only on allergic contact dermatitis. More information on the two other contact sensitivities is provided in the chapter on allergic skin diseases.

Allergic contact dermatitis occurs after a person is exposed to a specific chemical or substance, becomes sensitized, and then develops a rash if he or she should come into contact with that chemical or substance again. The rash, which may be red and swollen or blistery and scaly, will cause intense itching. An example is the rash caused by coming into contact with poison ivy, poison sumac, or poison oak.

Other common examples of contactants that can cause allergic contact dermatitis are hair dyes, fabric dyes, some jewelry, some perfumes, and some soaps.

It would be difficult to list all of the allergenic chemicals, or contactants, that are created to make our lives simpler or more beautiful. It is enough to say that when a rash occurs on a particular part of the body on which the contactant (such as a synthetic substance that is made with chemicals) is placed, and the rash disappears when the synthetic substance is removed, it is likely that the person had an allergic attack. If that substance were introduced again to the person in question and a rash reappeared, the allergy would be confirmed. The synthetic substance would then be considered the contactant or allergen.

# Asthma

The term *allergy* was first used in 1906. It referred to any unusual reaction, either helpful or harmful, within the immune system. Sixty years later, the IgE antibody was discovered, and its role in causing allergic symptoms was revealed.

Today, allergy is defined as a harmful increase in susceptibility to a particular substance or substances. With the increase in concern about the nature of our environment, particularly about pollutants that allow airborne allergens to remain in the air for longer periods, more attention has been paid to the allergic diseases. Nevertheless, the recognized types of allergic diseases and the way in which certain allergens affect various organs of the body has not changed over the years.

For purposes of clarity, we can classify allergic diseases by the organs they negatively affect. For instance, asthma is a disease of the lungs. Hay fever is a disease of the upper respiratory tract. Allergic diseases of the skin include *eczema* and some forms of dermatitis. Allergic diseases of the gastrointestinal tract include colic and other intestinal disturbances.

Asthma is a noncontagious disease of the lungs, more specifically, the bronchial tubes. Although asthma has been recognized as a medical condition since the time of Hippocrates and about 10 million people in the United States suffer from it, recent statistics point to a growth in death rates that is a source of concern to the National Heart, Lung and Blood Institute. According to Dr. Claude J. Lenfant, who is the director of the Institute, from 1979 to 1988, the death toll in the United States climbed from about two thousand to about four thousand each year. In addition, he points out that death rates from asthma are three times higher in blacks than in whites and increasing.

Some health officials have called this increase alarming because it is occurring during a time when death rates for other chronic diseases have been dropping. What is even more alarming, according to the National Heart, Lung and Blood Institute, is the fact that some of the deaths could have been avoided. A report recently issued by the Institute presented the first national guidelines for the diagnosis and treatment of this lung ailment. It was suggested that one cause for the increase in asthma deaths may be a lack of vigilance on the part of doctors, who must monitor patients.[1] Even mild cases can become serious if a prescribed treatment plan is not strictly followed.

It was not suggested that asthma sufferers could not lead normal, active lives, but it was strongly urged that this disease must not be taken lightly by doctors and their patients.

The bronchial tubes carry air from the mouth to the air sacs in the lungs. In the case of asthma, the bronchial tubes are obstructed by: swelling of the inside lining of the bronchial tubes; contraction of the muscles surrounding the tubes, thereby reducing their diameter; and secretion of thick *mucus*, which often hardens and forms plugs.

If we could see inside the body during the actual process of an asthma attack, we could understand why an episode can be unpleasant and sometimes very frightening.

Air inhaled through either the nose or the mouth is carried from the throat into the lungs by way of the trachea, or windpipe. The air then passes into the bronchial tubes and bronchioles (large and small airways) and finally into the *alveoli*, or air sacs.[2]

When an asthma attack occurs, the muscle that surrounds the bronchial tubes tightens so that it is difficult for the air to pass through to the air sacs. At the same time, the glands surrounding the bronchial tubes secrete a thick, sticky mucus that clogs the bronchioles. With the narrowing of the air passages, breathing is labored, and *wheezing* occurs with each effort to push the air through.

The exact cause of these three reactions is unknown. But the one characteristic that distinguishes asthma is what is called *hyperactive bronchial tubes*: the bronchial tubes react to certain stimuli in a way that induces the three abnormalities. Professionals often refer to the lungs of the asthmatic patient as "twitchy" because they overreact to stimuli that are usually harmless to the normal person.


## TRIGGERS OF AN ASTHMATIC ATTACK

Asthma can be triggered by allergic or nonallergic causes. Nonallergic asthma is usually caused by

- Viral infections
- Excessive exercise

- Changing weather conditions
- Strong irritating odors
- Air pollutants

Allergic asthma is usually caused by allergens such as

- Pollens
- Molds
- Animal danders
- House dust
- Some foods

Some people have a mixed form of asthma and react to both allergic and nonallergic triggers. Children have been known to have asthma attacks each time they contract an upper respiratory infection. Other people have asthma attacks only during certain times of the year, especially during spring and fall, the hay fever seasons. Some react to dusty environments and others to household chemicals. Still others may find that food loaded with preservatives such as sulfites may cause a severe asthma attack. However, it is unusual, though not unheard of, that food itself triggers an asthma attack. Strenuous or prolonged exercise, such as running, jogging, or aerobics, can cause an asthma attack. If exercises are performed when it is very warm or in areas with high humidity, the asthmatic symptoms can be aggravated.

Aspirin and other nonsteroidal anti-inflammatory drugs are dangerous, and asthmatic persons are particularly advised to avoid using them.

Air pollution, caused by carbon monoxide, sulfur dioxide, and other industrial airborne chemicals, as well as by tobacco smoke (even if it is inhaled secondhand), is extremely dangerous for asthma sufferers. When the air is particularly noxious, the departments of health in various towns and cities will issue an alert, especially to asthma sufferers, to stay indoors.

Despite its many causes and its disturbing symptoms, asthma can be controlled so that those who have it can live happily and function normally. In fact, asthma sufferers, who at one time were advised to "take it easy," feel much better if they are not singled out, especially if they are children. They prefer to lead active, ordinary lives. However, if asthmatic symptoms persist for longer than one day, a visit to the doctor is advised.

## THE PHYSICAL EXAM

At the doctor's office, a complete physical examination will be given, with particular attention paid to the nose and sinuses for signs of chronic infection. A *spirometer*, which measures the amount of air inhaled and exhaled, will be used to determine the level of airway obstruction. A chest X ray as well as a *skin test* will be given.[3]

A skin test consists of a series of slight scratches or pricks made on the skin. Certain allergens are then introduced into the scratch. If a red bump appears in the area where an allergen was introduced, the person is probably sensitive to that substance, and it may be the cause of the asthma attack.

Once the causes are discovered, the patient will be advised to avoid the irritants. This is very important, especially if it is found that an allergen such as mold or dust, drugs, or pollutants is the main cause of asthma attacks.

If an attack is brought on by exercising too rigorously, the exercise regimen should be modified or, if the attacks are particularly severe, eliminated entirely. Sometimes a medication to be used prior to exercising is prescribed.

If an asthma attack appears to be brought on by emotional stress, the person will have to learn ways to avoid situations that may produce stress. Certain breathing exercises that have been shown to help reduce stress levels may be recommended by the physician.

Though difficult, it is possible to reduce or even clear thickened mucus from affected air passages. Drinking two glasses of warm water, four times a day, has been successful in some cases. It has also been found that caffeine and some spicy foods assist in reducing a build-up of mucus.

Physicians can and do suggest various exercises for an asthma sufferer to perform during scheduled exercise periods or at the onset of attacks. Exercises of one to two minutes in length is usually recommended; airway obstruction increases when exercise is continued for more than five minutes.

## MANAGEMENT OF ASTHMA THROUGH MEDICATIONS

In the past ten years, dramatic improvements in asthma therapy have allowed a greater majority of asthma sufferers to lead fairly normal lives. The practice of using various medications rather than relying on just one medication to combat the effects of asthma is more commonplace.

Modern research has pointed positively to the release of more sophisticated medications in the very near future. For example, the discovery of leukotrienes, chemicals believed to be responsible for the more severe symptoms of asthma, has aided researchers in developing drugs that attempt to block their harmful effects. So far, these drugs have proved effective in preventing asthma attacks in animals, and testing on humans has already begun.

Child with asthma using an
inhaler to ease breathing

The following are some of the more common medications in present use.

*Cromolyn sodium*: This preventive medication is available in two forms. As a powder it is forced into the lungs by a special device called a Spinhaler. As a solution, it is inhaled through a kind of atomizer called a nebulizer. Cromolyn sodium suppresses the inflammatory response in the asthmatic sufferer. Because of its limited side effects, cromolyn sodium is safe for young children. Asthma sufferers can use this medication before they enter an environment that may cause irritation, but once an attack has begun, the medication is no longer helpful.

*Beta-adrenergic agents*: These medications are adrenaline-like agents that cause the airways to open. They can be administered orally, by aerosol, or by injection. Medications such as albuterol, metaproterenol, and terbutaline help the muscles relax but do not cause the heart to beat as fast as do other adrenaline-like medications.

*Theophylline*: This medication is frequently used in the drug therapy of asthma patients. It is known as a *bronchodilator* because it relaxes the bronchial muscles. It also stimulates the cilia, tiny hairlike projections lining the airways, so that mucus is kept out of the lungs. Theophylline can also strengthen the lungs and diaphragm so that asthma attacks are less severe. Sustained-release theophylline is especially effective in controlling asthma attacks at night.

*Corticosteroids*: If other medications have been tried and found to be ineffective, steroids, derived from the hormone cortisone, are used by those with severe cases of asthma. Given orally, they are extremely effective because they decrease the buildup of mucus in the bronchial tubes and are known to reduce inflammation. However, corticosteroids have many side effects. Such reactions as weight gain, high blood pressure, cataracts, swelling, muscle weakness, insomnia, or weakened bones are not uncommon.

The side effects can be reduced or even eliminated by using smaller dosages over a less concentrated period. Short-acting corticosteroid preparations include prednisone, prednisolone, and methylprednisolone. Inhaled corticosteroids are very helpful, and sometimes side effects are avoided when the medication is administered by this method.

*Nedocromil*: One of the newer drugs that can treat asthma symptoms in a short time without any dangerous side effects, it can be administered through a handheld inhaler four times a day. According to studies at the National Jewish Center for Immunology and Respiratory Diseases, Nedocromil may actually prevent asthma from occuring.

*Immunotherapy*: This treatment involves periodic injections of the allergens (pollen, dust, molds) that cause the asthma attacks. Each successive injection is in greater concentrations, with the goal of allowing the body to build up a resistance to asthma-triggering substances.

## ASTHMA AND THE EMOTIONS

A common misconception is that there is a psychological relationship between anxiety, emotional flare-ups, or stress and the onset of asthma. It is thought that a person who suffers from asthma may be in some way emotionally disturbed. Additionally, some believe that those who suffer from asthma are lazy, that they are afraid to do anything because the activity might cause an attack. Worse than that, children who suffer from asthma are even thought to be victims of a domineering mother or are "crybabies" or "mama's boys." There have been many studies to determine the validity of these views.

The final verdict is that there is little evidence to

substantiate any of these claims. Emotional anxiety and stress can cause fatigue, which may be responsible for worsening the symptoms of asthma, but these are usually secondary factors in provoking an asthma attack. There is no evidence of an asthmatic personality or profile. And it never has been proved that a domineering mother can cause asthma.[4]

Although these ideas are obviously incorrect, there have been many cases of asthma sufferers who were stigmatized by such prejudices; therefore, it is important to dispel them. Most asthma sufferers, once on a regular medical regimen, prove to be normal, productive individuals.

# Allergic Skin Diseases

The skin is the body's largest organ, and when anything happens to it, the results are easily seen. In the case of allergic skin diseases, the symptoms are not only visible, they are usually uncomfortable. Unfortunately, the chances are that an allergic skin disease will develop if a person has other allergies.

## ECZEMA

Eczema, or *atopic dermatitis*, is an allergic condition that usually appears as small, crusty, dry patches in the bends of elbows, at the backs of knees, behind the ears, or on the face and neck. Because it is accompanied by severe itching, the scratching that follows will cause the rash to ooze or "weep," allowing bacteria to enter and cause infection. When the rashes dry, they often become dark, purplish, thickened, or even leathery. If the itching could be controlled, the rashes would eventually disappear. But it is almost impossible not to scratch.

Eczema affects about 3 percent of all children,

especially those who have a hereditary tendency toward hay fever or asthma. According to statistics, nearly half of those who suffer from eczema develop hay fever, and one-third are asthmatic.

Eczema usually appears in infancy and looks like chapped skin on the scalp, forehead, and cheeks. If not treated quickly, the rash can spread to the trunk, arms, and legs. The condition causes irritability, restlessness, and sleeplessness in infants. Sixty percent of all cases of eczema appear before age one, the remainder of the cases appearing by the age of five. Though most sufferers lose their eczema before adulthood, those who do not may have a tendency toward hyperactivity. During childhood, those who suffer from this skin condition may exhibit behavioral problems. They may tend to become loners or to "act out" in the classroom and at home. And who could really blame someone who is so embarrassed by this condition that he or she tends to stay away from people? By the same token, it is not hard to imagine that a child with eczema may call attention to himself by misbehaving and distracting people so that they forget about his embarrassing condition.

The exact cause of eczema is uncertain. Some foods, especially milk and milk products; airborne allergens like dust, pollen, and animal dander; and sometimes psychological stress have been linked to its onset.

Before it can be determined that a person is suffering from eczema, other skin disorders should be ruled out.

Tinea dermatitis is caused by a variety of fungal agents. Tinea pedis, or athlete's foot, is a form of skin irritation of which most people are aware. Other examples of skin irritations caused by fungal agents are tinea capitis, or ringworm of the scalp, and tinea circinata, which is ringworm of the face, neck, and arms.

Pityriasis rosea is another skin condition that can often be confused with eczema. It appears as raised, salmon-colored rashes on the trunk of the body. It can be distinguished by the herald patch, a quarter- to a half-dollar-size rash on the chest or back. This condition causes no itching.

Once similar skin disorders are removed from consideration, the doctor continues by looking for

- Intense itch
- Reddened rashes localized in single dry patches or generalized about the body
- "Weeping" rash
- Rash located mainly on cheeks, neck, and sometimes scalp, arms, legs, and trunk
- Family history of allergy

The diagnosis of eczema is also made on the basis of a complete medical history and a thorough physical examination. Blood tests will reveal abnormally high IgE antibody levels in almost 100 percent of the people who have eczema. Skin tests are usually not used as a diagnostic tool because the skin is already irritated.

Most doctors would agree that the best approach to the treatment of eczema is environmental control. In the home, substances that tend to cause allergic symptoms—feathers, dust, animal dander, and some plants—should be removed. The skin of a person suffering from eczema will become more itchy and irritated when the indoor air is dry. A humidifier would be helpful to avoid this situation.

A simple elimination diet for a trial period using certain foods, such as milk, eggs, and wheat, which are common food allergens, may be tried to determine whether those allergens are the cause of the eczema. As a general rule, if the food is removed for about two weeks and the rashes disappear, it is possible that the food in question is causing the problem. But to make sure, the food may be reintroduced to the diet. If the rash reappears, the likelihood is that the tested food is in fact the trigger of eczema.

It is also important that a person who suffers from eczema be kept away from stressful situations whenever possible. It is thought that stress may intensify the condition.

### Treatment

The most important treatment in managing eczema is to stop the itching. There are many varieties of antihistamine medications available; they are taken orally because it would not be wise to treat the irritated skin directly with a compound that is known to cause irritations itself. Benadryl, Atarax, and Periactin are examples of effective oral antihistamines.

The skin of a person suffering from eczema should also be lubricated because well-moisturized skin is less itchy. However, some lubricants can be more harmful than helpful. For instance, if a person is allergic to wool, then lanolin would not be good to use because it is derived from sheep. One of the most effective and least expensive lubricants can probably be found in food pantries. Vegetable shortenings, such as Crisco, though very greasy, are quite effective.

## CONTACT DERMATITIS _____

Contact dermatitis is characterized by skin eruptions caused by substances that come into *direct* contact with the skin. The condition appears in three main forms:

- Allergic contact dermatitis—a rash that develops as an allergic reaction to something that touches the skin. Poison ivy is the most common type of allergic contact dermatitis. It is estimated that seven out of ten Americans are allergic to urushiol, an oily resin that is the allergen causing the reaction to poison ivy. Symptoms are an itchy red rash on the areas of the skin that were touched by the plant. Blisters and swelling can also develop. Unlike eczema, the rash will not spread unless a wider area of skin came into contact with the allergen. In addition to poison ivy, allergies to other plants, to chemicals, to cosmetics, and to drugs can cause allergic contact dermatitis. Of course, as with all other allergies, the person must be sensitized first. He or she won't get the rashes and itch the first time, but if the skin is touched by the allergen after the first time, the rashes and itching will surface.

- Irritant contact dermatitis—a rash that is not caused by an allergen but by contact with a strong irritant, such as a cleaning product or a chemical. Diaper rash, caused by ammonia in the urine, is a classic example
- Photoallergic contact dermatitis—an unusual condition in which a reaction occurs between a specific chemical and exposure to the ultraviolet rays of the sun, producing a rash. Both conditions must be present for the reaction to occur, so it is relatively rare. These skin conditions are not the result of an allergy.

Management of contact dermatitis, whether allergic or not, usually follows the same treatment procedure: application of cool, wet compresses and perhaps a cortisone cream to the affected area to reduce the inflammation and itch. Antihistamine creams, lotions, and ointments are not advised because they may cause another contact dermatitis and make matters even worse. Sometimes, in severe cases, the doctor may prescribe oral or injected steroids. Preventative measures include wearing protective gloves or clothing if

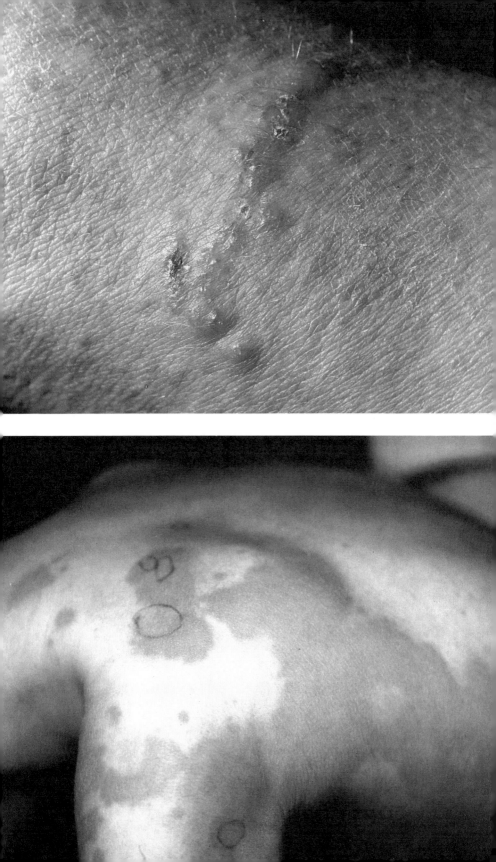

exposure is anticipated and washing clothing and skin immediately after exposure.

## HIVES AND ANGIOEDEMA _____

Hives, known medically as *urticaria*, erupt on the surface of the skin as well-outlined raised areas with a reddish or whitish coloration. There is no standard size for hives. They can be as small as drops of water or so large they cover an entire arm or leg. Hives can appear on any part of the body and can develop internally along the length of the intestinal tract.

The numbers of hives and their location vary. An attack can consist of one large hive, many hives located in different parts of the body, or a group of many small hives concentrated in a specific part of the body. Sometimes the hives will grow together, forming a single large swelling. Lesions of this kind are called giant hives.

Hives also itch intensely. As a rule, eruptions of hives will appear without warning and then slowly subside. Sometimes, however, hives may be present for a longer period. Hives that recur for six weeks or more are defined as chronic; those that recur for six weeks or less are defined as acute.

It is estimated that 10 to 20 percent of the population will suffer from hives at one time or another. Acute hives appear more frequently in persons who are allergy-prone, whereas chronic hives can strike both those who are allergic and those who are not.

*Angioedema* is a hive that has invaded the deeper

(Top) Poison-ivy rash
(Bottom) Hives can result from
exposure to certain drugs,
infections, foods, and insects.

tissues of the skin. It spreads across the skin and seems to be borderless. Even though angioedema is a hive, it does not itch. Itching is produced by nerves located in the outer skin layers. Since angioedema invades the deeper skin layers, the superficial nerve endings are not affected. The extreme swelling of the angioedema frequently causes pain, especially in areas of the body where the skin is stretched. If angioedema involves areas such as the tongue, mouth, or windpipe (the trachea), it can be dangerous, because the swelling can impede breathing.

### How Hives Happen
Hives develop when the chemical mediator histamine is secreted into the blood stream and body tissues. Histamine can be released through many mechanisms, but the most common is an allergic reaction. No matter how the histamine is released, the end result is the same: leakage of fluid out of the small blood vessels, swelling, skin eruptions, and intense itching. Hives can be triggered by drugs, infections, foods, insects, and, physical agents; in some cases they are of undiscovered cause.

Hives can develop because of an allergic reaction or intolerance to drugs. Some of the drugs responsible for the development of hives include antibiotics, aspirin, barbiturates, codeine, insulin, iodides, penicillin, sulfa drugs, and tetanus antitoxin.

Many allergists believe that a small percentage of hives episodes may be caused by low-grade infections of the tonsils, adenoids, sinuses, teeth, gall bladder, or urinary tract.

Food and food additives are common causes of hives. Some of the most frequent offenders are dairy products, eggs, peanuts, nuts, citrus fruits, tomatoes, and shellfish. In addition to tartrazine and benzoic acid, such food additives as sulfites and metabisulfites can cause hives.

Acute hives are likely to be triggered by seasonal or unusual foods, such as strawberries or shellfish, whereas chronic hives are likely to result from foods that are part of the daily diet, such as wheat, milk, and eggs. Usually hives appear immediately after eating an offending food, but sometimes they don't appear for as much as eighteen to twenty-four hours.

Though insect-induced hives are most often triggered by the members of the Hymenoptera order, such as bees, wasps, and hornets, several other flying and crawling creatures can be responsible as well.

Other common types of hives and angioedema include the following:

- Papular urticaria—a hivelike eruption found on the lower extremities is caused by bites from bedbugs, fleas, or mites. The lesions are very itchy, smaller in size, and hard to get rid of. A rash known as caterpillar dermatitis is caused by contact with exactly what you might suppose, a caterpillar. In the northeastern United States, the gypsy moth caterpillar causes the rash.
- Dermatrophism—hivelike lesions on skin that has been physically written on or rubbed.
- Cold urticaria—hives caused by sudden exposure to the cold. This condition can sometimes be accompanied by headache, wheezing, and, rarely, breathing problems.
- Cholinergic urticaria—hives caused by emotional stress, heavy physical exertion, or heat exposure. The rash consists of many small lesions and is quite itchy.
- Localized heat urticaria—hives developed as a result of exposure of skin surfaces that are locally heated or heated in one spot and not all over the body, for example, by a sun lamp or a flame.
- Solar urticaria—hives caused by sunlight when

certain areas of the skin are directly and repeatedly exposed.

- Vibratory angioedema—swelling of the skin when it comes in contact with a vibrating object such as a throttle or jackhammer. This condition is thought to be rare and probably inherited.
- Pressure urticaria and angioedema—caused when persistent pressure is applied to various parts of the body. Tight clothes, shoes, women's undergarments, and elastic socks can cause this condition. Oddly enough, the resulting hives and swellings can appear up to four to six hours after the pressure has ceased.
- Exercise-induced urticaria—hives or angioedema that appears after periods of strenuous physical exercise.
- Urticaria pigmentosa—a rare condition in which there are elevated, localized pigmented hives. Underneath the hives are mast cells, the white blood cells that carry histamine. If these areas are rubbed or even touched, histamine will be released, and hives will form. Children who are affected by this skin disorder usually outgrow it.

The appearance of hives can also, in some cases, indicate problems with muscle and connective tissue, the early stages of rheumatoid arthritis, or endocrine system disorders.

The best treatment for hives is to avoid the substances or situations that cause them. However, there are some effective medications available, such as Atarax, Vistaril, Benadryl, and Periactin, which are antihistamines. For sudden episodes of hives or angioedema, *epinephrine* is often helpful. Corticosteroids are used when conditions persist and no other medications seem to work.

# Hay Fever/Rhinitis

Technically speaking, *rhinitis* is an inflammation of the *mucous membrane* of the nose. The term "chronic" is derived from the Greek *kronos*, or time. Chronic rhinitis is an inflammation of the nose, causing sneezing, runny nose, coughing—all of the miserable symptoms of a cold. But these symptoms are not caused by a virus, nor do the symptoms disappear in about a week, as they do with a cold.

Cassidy Clune experienced this problem when he began to attend kindergarten. First Cassidy did have a cold. Then he had another cold, it seemed. But the symptoms did not disappear and over the course of time, the symptoms got worse before they got better. And they got better only when the weather cooled.

The major forms of rhinitis are

- Seasonal allergic rhinitis—commonly known as hay fever (the "cold" Cassidy didn't have).
- Perennial allergic rhinitis—like hay fever but with symptoms year-round.

- Vasomotor rhinitis—a year-round nonallergic, noninfectious form of chronic rhinitis caused by an imbalance in the mechanism that controls the nasal mucous membranes. Such conditions as temperature change, irritating odors, or emotional stress can trigger an overreaction in the nasal membranes.
- Infectious rhinitis—another term for the common cold.
- Rhinitis medicamentosa—an inflammation of the mucous membranes caused by abuse of nose drops or sprays.

## SEASONAL ALLERGIC RHINITIS _____

Commonly called hay fever, this form of rhinitis is characterized by a seasonal pattern of recurring symptoms triggered by an allergy to the pollen of weeds, trees, grasses, and mold spores. Depending on where you live in the United States, the hay fever season can begin in mid-March and can extend through mid-October, possibly with a break in July and August. Though plants may end pollen production in mid-October, pollen may continue to exist in the air until it is killed off with the first frost. This is the reason some hay fever sufferers continue to have symptoms through November and early December.[1]

Symptoms common to hay fever include

- Violent sneezing spells.
- Itching, tearing eyes.
- Watery, clear, nonirritating nasal discharge.
- Nasal congestion, nose itching and rubbing.
- Itching in the ears, mouth, and throat.
- Dark circles under the eyes during allergy season.

- Mouth breathing and clearing of the throat.
- Reduction in the sense of smell.

Some people become irritable, listless, and gloomy, and who would blame them? During the season when most of us are outdoors enjoying the warm weather, at least 20 million people, including Cassidy, must be very careful before stepping outside. Some sufferers may miss work. In fact, annually, $154 million is lost in wages not collected by people who suffered hay fever attacks and had to stay home.

An interesting study in relation to hay fever sufferers and the fact that they may often miss work was conducted by Dr. Iris Bell, a University of Arizona psychiatrist. She was able to correlate shyness with allergies. In the study, 375 students from universities across the country were divided into four groups—from extremely shy to extremely outgoing. Researchers found that the shyest group also were more likely to suffer from allergies, particularly hay fever. While it can be agreed that hay fever does not cause shyness, a possible conclusion may be that some symptoms of allergic rhinitis, such as coughing, sneezing, and wheezing, may be annoying to other people. If people with allergies continually feel that their symptoms are annoying other people, it is possible to imagine that they might be reluctant to socialize with others and therefore consider themselves shy.

There are two types of medication commonly used to provide relief for hay fever sufferers: antihistamines, which prevent the symptoms from occurring, and *decongestants*, which work after the symptoms have begun. The negative side effect of these medications is drowsiness. Some new antihistamines, available by prescription, work effectively and do not cause drowsiness. Terfenadine is one antihistamine on the market (under

the brand name Seldane) that does not produce drowsiness. Astemizole is another; it is taken only once a day. Beclomethasone and flunisolide are two cortisone-based medications that help to reduce inflammation; although they are not new, they are still prescribed because they are very effective.

## PERENNIAL ALLERGIC RHINITIS

Having perennial allergic rhinitis is like having hay fever all year long. However, the allergens triggering the symptoms of this condition are not just pollens. Such allergens as dust, animal dander, wool, and mold spores from indoor plants can be the culprits. Antihistamines and decongestants usually provide some relief. In addition, careful observation to detect a possible link to an allergen, and the removal of the offender, may provide relief.

## VASOMOTOR OR NONALLERGIC RHINITIS

This condition is caused by an imbalance in the nervous system controlling the production of mucus in the nasal membranes. Vasomotor rhinitis is not caused by either an allergy or a virus. Changes in air temperature and humidity levels, strong or irritating odors, tobacco smoke, or emotional stress stimulate the nerves controlling the blood vessels within the nose. The blood flow will decrease, resulting in nasal congestion.

Vasomotor rhinitis is different from other forms of rhinitis. There is no pattern of symptoms appearing

(Top) Sneezing is a common
hay-fever symptom.
(Bottom) Ragweed

throughout the year, and sneezing or itching of the eyes, ears, and throat are usually absent. Medical treatment such as the standard antihistamines and decongestants are not as effective for those who suffer from the vasomotor form of rhinitis. Some prescription drugs or a nasal steroid spray, such as Nasalide, Beconase, or Vancenase may help. Avoidance of tobacco smoke and/or strong, irritating odors is always advised.[2]

## INFECTIOUS RHINITIS

Infectious rhinitis is the common cold. It can be distinguished from other forms of rhinitis because it lasts only from one week to ten days. There are other ways to distinguish a cold from an allergy. In addition to nasal congestion, there is a nasal discharge that can be yellow or green in color, which indicates an infection is in progress. This discharge is very irritating and causes the usual redness of the nostrils and upper lip. Coughing, fever, stomach upset, body aches, and fatigue may accompany this nasal disorder.

Although antihistamines and decongestants can provide some relief, they aren't quite as effective as for allergic rhinitis. Lots of fluids, aspirin, some bed rest, and—believe it or not—chicken soup will ease the symptoms until the cold passes.[3]

## RHINITIS MEDICAMENTOSA

With so many nasal sprays and nose drops readily available to the allergy sufferer, it is not hard to abuse them. In fact, when nasal sprays or nose drops are used too frequently, they lose their effectiveness. When this happens, the allergy sufferer increases the usage even further. Eventually, the sprays and drops will worsen the symptoms they were supposed to stop.

Now the sufferer has to increase the dosage of nasal sprays or nose drops to prevent or control symptoms caused by the drops or sprays themselves. It becomes a vicious cycle.

When symptoms are caused by the medications that were originally used to alleviate the symptoms of an allergy, the condition is known as rhinitis medicamentosa. The only cure for this predicament is to discontinue the use of sprays and drops completely.

## COMPLICATIONS FROM FORMS OF RHINITIS _____

### Sinusitis

Sinusitis is an inflammation of the sinuses. The sinuses are cavities located behind the nose and below the eyes. There are four pairs of sinuses, named for the facial and cranial bones near them: ethmoid, maxillary, frontal, and sphenoid.

Although there is no complete agreement about what specific function the sinuses perform, it is generally believed that they are involved with our sense of smell and the production of mucus secretions. It is also thought that the sinuses may play a part in voice control and, since the sinuses are hollow, reduce the weight of the head.

Sinuses are lined with the same tissue that lines the nose. They open into the back of the nose by small openings called *sinus ostia*. Most people are not aware of the sinuses, but when an allergic reaction occurs, involving the membranes of the nose, sinus membranes can swell and overflow with mucus. If that happens, the drainage openings can become blocked. Fluid will be trapped. This situation can cause a buildup of pressure and that pressure can cause some very painful headaches. The trapped mucus provides an environment in which bacteria and viruses can multiply, which can lead to sinusitis. Sinusitis includes symptoms of fever, chills, severe headaches, dizziness, and secretion of a thick, greenish mucus.

The treatment for this very unpleasant condition generally involves oral decongestants, antihistamines, and, when infection is present, antibiotics. Nasal drops or sprays can be used to dry the sinus membranes, but they are not recommended for longer than five days. In some cases, when sinusitis persists and the usual forms of treatment are not effective, surgery may be called for to open a permanent drainage passageway between the sinus and the nose in order to prevent further accumulations of mucus.[4]

### Nosebleeds

The possibility of nosebleeds increases whenever chronic nasal symptoms appear. Chronic rhinitis often causes irritation, and occasionally the blood vessels surrounding the nasal membranes may rupture. Sometimes the tissues are so delicate that a little sneeze will cause bleeding. During cold weather, when household heating may dry out the lining of the nose, the possibility of bleeding increases. If nosebleeds persist, even when a humidifier is used to keep the lining of the nose moist, it is time to see a doctor. The doctor can usually stop the bleeding with a chemical or an electric probe to the vessel that has been bleeding. The treatment is effective and painless.

### Changes in the Dental Arch

Children who suffer from chronic rhinitis and nasal congestion frequently become mouth breathers. If unchecked, breathing through the mouth can cause permanent changes in the shape of the mouth. The result may be a higher-arched palate, which can stop the upper and lower jaw from meeting properly. If that happens, extensive orthodontic work may be required.

# Ear and Eye Allergies

It has been estimated that about one-half of all children have had an earache at least once. Boys, obese children, and allergy-prone children tend to be most susceptible. Earaches can be the result of an infection in the middle ear, also known as otitis media. Otitis media is not caused by an allergy.

The most common symptom of acute otitis media is the sudden onset of severe ear pain, usually associated with a fever. Sometimes the pain is so strong that the sufferer may cry out and become extremely irritable. Treatment with an antibiotic over a period of ten days to two weeks will usually cure the problem.

Secretory otitis media, sometimes called serous otitis media, is sometimes linked to allergies and is common in people, especially children, who suffer from allergic rhinitis. It seems the swollen mucous membranes can extend into the area where the *eustachian tube* opens into the nasopharynx. Depending on the amount of swelling, the mouth of the eustachian tube may become partially or completely blocked. The blockage interferes with the normal drainage of ear fluid, which then becomes trapped. Since the fluid itself does not cause pain and is not irritating, large amounts can accumulate. People affected by this allergic earache complain that they feel as if they were hearing underwater.

Usually, treatment consists of using decongestants and antihistamines. If the condition persists, a physician may perform a simple drainage procedure. Sometimes drainage tubes are placed in the affected ear. In some cases surgery may be recommended to remove the adenoids if they are contributing to the problem. If there is a definite association between earaches and allergies, the home environment should also be taken into consideration. To avoid the onset of earaches, precautionary steps such as keeping the home dust-free and humid, especially during the winter season, will help.

## OCULAR (EYE) ALLERGIES

For some people who suffer from allergic rhinitis, or hay fever, the period from the middle of August to the middle of October may present symptoms that can almost drive them crazy. Every morning they awake with swollen eyelids. Their eyes itch constantly and sometimes swell when they go outdoors.

The acute form of *allergic conjunctivitis* produces sudden swelling of the *conjunctiva*, the outer covering of the eye. This is accompanied by redness and heavy tearing. Either one or both eyes can be affected. Sometimes a sufferer can be extremely sensitive to light, a condition known as photophobia. The chronic form of allergic conjunctivitis produces symptoms that make the eyes itchy and dry with blurry vision and increased sensitivity to light. In addition, the conjunctiva may have a finely granular or roughened appearance.

Treatment for the acute and chronic types of aller-

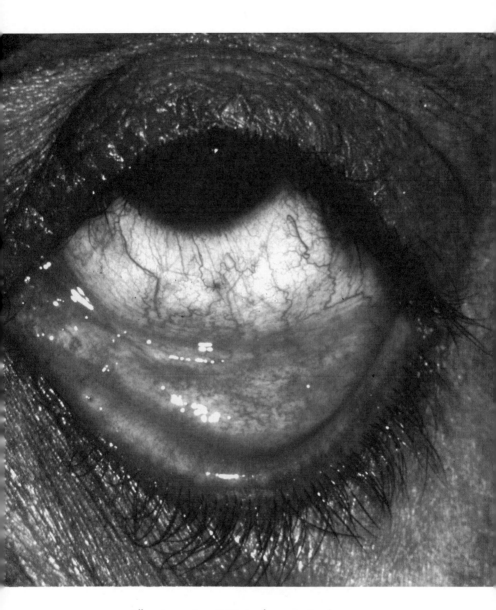

Allergic conjunctivitis is characterized
by swelling of the outer covering
of the eye (the conjunctiva) and by
redness and heavy tearing.

gic conjunctivitis consists of eye drops that contain such drugs as phenylephrine, tetrahydrozoline, and naphazoline. Steroid-based drops or ointments are also effective. However, it is recommended that such medicines not be used over an extended period without some monitoring by an eye doctor (ophthalmologist). Oral antihistamines can also be used to control the symptoms. Opticrom (cromolyn sodium in a 4 percent solution) is one of the more promising medications now available, but it must be administered as a preventive medicine to be effective.

## Vernal Conjunctivitis

One form of conjunctivitis affects sufferers in the spring and summer months and is relatively uncommon. It is called vernal conjunctivitis and primarily affects children. The symptoms include severe itching of both eyes and the sensation that there is something in the eyes. In fact, if the inner part of the upper eyelid is lifted, small, hard stonelike bumps can be seen. Other symptoms include blurred vision and extreme light sensitivity. Topical steroids, carefully monitored by an ophthalmologist, are generally used to ease the discomfort.

## Conjunctivitis Related to Atopic Dermatitis

In this form of conjunctivitis, the eyelids are thick and very dry. Occasionally, there may be wet lesions. The itching is more severe than the itching associated with conjunctivitis due to hay fever. In some cases, ulcers, or inflamed sores, and cataracts, a filmlike covering, can form on the cornea. But these cases are extremely rare. The most effective treatments involve the use of steroids and cromolyn sodium.

Contact dermatitis, an itchy, scaly rash that is caused by an irritating substance or chemical touching the skin, can sometimes affect the lids of the eyes. One of the main causes of contact dermatitis of the eyelids is the use of *eye* makeup. The best treatment is to discontinue the use of the offending makeup and substitute a nonallergenic makeup when the rash clears up. If the rash persists, a steroid ointment may be applied.

### Atopic Keratoconjunctivitis

Atopic keratoconjunctivitis is associated with atopic dermatitis, or eczema. It is most common in men between the ages of twenty-five and fifty. It is complicated by secondary infections that can decrease vision by affecting the cornea. With this condition, the eye never appears normal. The lids are thickened and hardened, and the skin around the eye is scaly.

# Seeing the Doctor

When his mother first realized that Cassidy was exhibiting certain symptoms that weren't necessarily those of a common cold, she might have created a list or a diary of the symptoms to see if there were any patterns that might seem significant. Did Cassidy develop a rash when he ate certain foods? Did he sneeze and yet show no other symptoms consistent with the common cold? Did his eyes itch during the early spring? Why did he start coughing every time she cleaned the carpets?

Depending on her findings, Cassidy's Mom could have made two choices:

> Choice No. 1: Cassidy's symptoms weren't making him that uncomfortable, so an over-the counter (nonprescription) medicine was all that was needed. Choice No. 2: The symptoms appeared frequently and made Cassidy so uncomfortable that a visit to the doctor seemed wise.

If we assume that Cassidy's symptoms warranted a

visit to his physician, then a visit should be made to determine the cause and provide the treatment to relieve Cassidy's symptoms. Cassidy would then join the ranks of the 30 million to 40 million allergy sufferers who are treated by their family doctors. If the symptoms seem beyond the generalized knowledge of a family doctor, then a doctor who has been specifically trained to diagnose and treat allergies should be seen.

## THE VISIT

Whenever anyone goes to an allergist, it is wise to be well-prepared. Cassidy's mother and father should know when their son first showed symptoms of an allergic attack. They should try to pin down such information as what he ate, what unusual clothing he wore, where he was at the time, and how long the reaction lasted.

Cassidy's parents should also be prepared to provide their own and their children's medical histories.

After the preliminary information is discussed, the allergist will perform a complete physical examination: taking blood pressure; measuring height and weight; checking eyes, ears, nose, and throat; and listening to the heart and lungs. Very often, the information given by Cassidy's parents, combined with the results of the physical examination and the observations made by the allergist while examining Cassidy, may be enough to offer a tentative diagnosis.

However, if the findings are inconclusive, the doctor will require specific tests. These tests, which are relatively painless, include the following:

- Blood tests to determine the hemoglobin level, the strength of the immune system, and the level of IgE protein.
- RAST, radioallergosorbent tests, to measure the sensitivity to individual allergens.

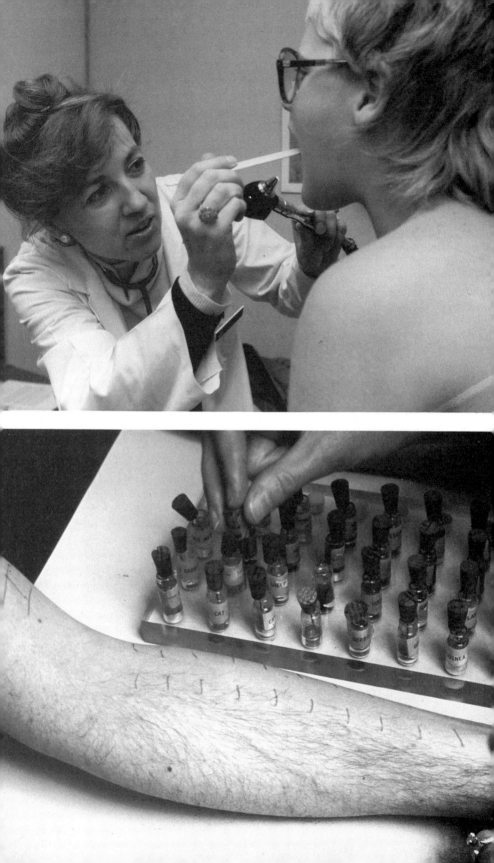

- PRIST, or paper radioimmunosorbent tests, to determine the amount of circulating IgE.
- X rays of the lungs to investigate blockages of the air passages, the sinuses, the upper and lower intestinal tract (possibly adding barium to follow the path of digestion, when food allergies are suspected).
- Pulmonary function studies to determine how efficiently the lungs are working.
- Epicutaneous (skin) tests, commonly called scratch tests, to determine sensitivity to specific allergens. Swelling or redness indicates a sensitivity to specific substances.
- Intracutaneous or intradermal tests, the most common type of testing. The process includes rows of injections administered within the skin's layers to determine sensitivity to specific allergens.
- Patch tests, in which patches of the suspected allergens are applied directly to the skin to see if there is a reaction of itching, swelling, or redness.
- Oral food *challenge tests* to prove a particular food causes sensitivity by systematically eliminating specific foods from the diet.

(Top) You should prepare for a visit to an allergy doctor by determining as many specific details of your allergic reaction as possible. These include the possible allergens to which you were exposed and the time of onset of the symptoms. (Bottom) The scratch test is used to determine sensitivity to different allergens.

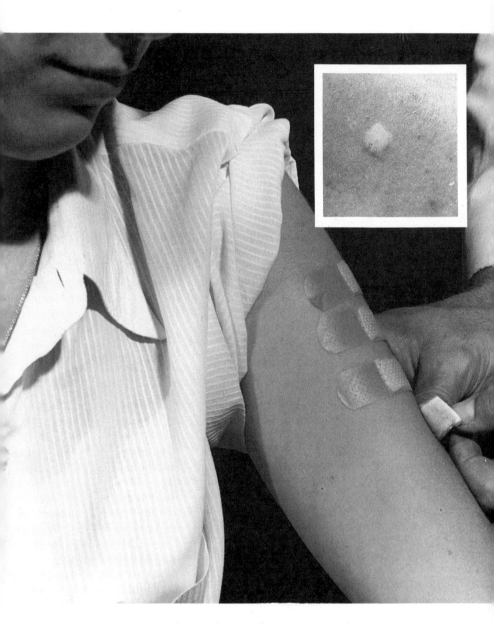

In the patch test, allergens are applied
directly to the skin to test for a reaction.
Inset: A positive reaction

Recording patient
reactions to certain
allergens

## DIAGNOSIS

When all tests have been completed, Cassidy, his parents, and his doctor will have gotten to know each other very well. As the diagnosis is provided, a program to eliminate the presence of allergens in Cassidy's life is instituted. In Cassidy's case, it started with giving away his dog. However, a program to provide the proper environment for Cassidy does not stop with giving away a pet.

If one of the allergens is dust, Cassidy's parents must try to eliminate as much dust as possible from the home by thorough cleaning; substitute synthetic fibers in furniture, clothing, and bedding stuffed with feathers; and use air conditioners, humidifiers, dehumidifiers, and vaporizers. If a food allergen is the culprit, that food must be eliminated from the diet.

Finally, the allergist may recommend the cutting back of some physical activity and suggest the use of antihistamines, decongestants, corticosteroids, and other medications to relieve discomfort.

Armed with good judgment, sound advice, proper medication, and the knowledge that life goes on even with allergies, the wise patient lives life the best he or she can.

## CLINICAL ECOLOGY

Recently, much attention has been focused on people who suffer from multiple chemical sensitivities (MCS). For these people, living life the best way they can means not very much good living. For those sufferers the simplest chores and pleasures in life are agony: going for a walk, visiting friends, shopping, seeing a movie, riding in a car or bus, even buying a newspaper have become painful. Among the symptoms attributed to these chemical allergies or sensitivities are fatigue, depression, headache, dizziness, irritability, nausea, rashes, watery eyes, asthma, nasal congestion, fatigue, mood swings, constipation, memory loss, and muscle and joint aches. All are common symptoms that can stem from any number of physical or emotional conditions, including anxiety, fear, and depression.

This condition, also known as environmental illness, total allergy syndrome, or twentieth-century illness, is caused, according to some physicians, by allergies to food, low levels of environmental pollutants in the air, and/or chemicals used in the manufacture of synthetic fabrics and other man-made materials.

Most allergists and scientists are baffled. They consider the diagnosis unscientific and unproven, saying there is little clinical evidence of immune system dysfunction or allergies. They lean more to the proposition that these so-called environmental illnesses are psychiatric disorders.

Nevertheless, the people who suffer from this syndrome have turned to a new medical specialty—clinical ecology—to relieve their symptoms. The treatment is harsh: The sufferers may have to live alone in a chemical-free, sealed-off environment and have very little contact with other people unless those people have thoroughly cleansed themselves. There can be no deodorants, perfume, dry-cleaned clothing, smoking, and probably, in this environment, no physical interaction at all. For those sufferers, life doesn't hold much fun. Until such time as this medical specialty has been scientifically validated, people who need to see doctors because they have symptoms of hay fever, eczema, or other allergic diseases would be wise to visit a conventional allergist first.

## FUTURE PROSPECTS

Lately, the term "allergy" has been misused to explain occurrences that have very little to do with an actual allergic reaction. For instance, some people have taken the liberty of using the term "allergic" to explain why they may not like certain other people or activities. They use it to explain a headache whose cause may have nothing to do with an allergy. Some behavior problems of children and even some actions of adults are often explained as an allergic reaction without proving such a reaction has taken place. Clinical ecologists claim that foods, pollutants, and chemicals are responsible for a wide range of allergic symptoms even though no tests have shown an allergic reaction.

Allergy has a very specific meaning: an abnormal immune system reaction to substances that are ordinarily harmless. To use the term indiscriminately can result in the perception that true allergy sufferers are malingerers or are trying to avoid responsibilities. Also, declaring that people can be allergic to television or to microwaves, as clinical ecologists do, may trivialize allergic conditions to the point where sufferers think they really don't have to take care of themselves.

In the case of Cassidy Jonathan Clune, hay fever symptoms are more annoying than dangerous. But if Cassidy is not monitored on a regular basis, his annoying symptoms can turn into painful events. A simple sneeze can develop into an excruciating earache.

While allergy sufferers should be careful to maintain their health, it does not follow that they cannot lead normal lives. In fact, most people are like Cassidy. They accept their condition and learn to live comfortably with it. The future is very promising in terms of new research and the development of new medications and therapies to make life easier for those who suffer from sneezes, wheezes, itches, and rashes, and a host of other symptoms of an allergy.

# Where to Write
# for More Information

If you are interested in additional information about allergies, you might want to write to one of the following agencies. To be sure the information you request gets to you, include a stamped, self-addressed envelope.

American Academy of Allergy and Immunology
611 East Wells Street
Milwaukee, WI 53202

American Allergy Association
P.O. Box 7273
Menlo Park, CA 94026

Asthma and Allergy Foundation of America
1302 18th Street, NW
Suite 30
Washington, DC 20036

Asthma Project
National Heart, Lung and Blood Institute
Building 31, Room 4A-21
Bethesda, MD 20205

National Center for Health Statistics
National Institutes of Health
Building 31, Room 7A32
Bethesda, MD 20892

National Institute of Allergy and Infectious Diseases
National Institutes of Health
Bethesda, MD 20205

American Association of Certified Allergists
401 East Prospect Avenue
Suite 210
Mount Prospect, IL 60056

American College of Allergists
800 East Northwest Highway
Suite 101
Mount Prospect, IL 60056

American Association for Clinical Immunology
and Allergy
P.O. Box 912
Omaha, NE 68101

# Source Notes

CHAPTER 1 _____

1. Material on the chemistry of an allergic reaction
   was developed from M. Eric Gershwin, M.D., and
   Edwin L. Klingelhofer, Ph.D., *Conquering Your
   Children's Allergies* (Reading, MA: Addison-
   Wesley, 1989), pp. 6–8; Donald Vickery, M.D.,
   and James Fries, M.D., *Take Care of Yourself*
   (Reading, MA: Addison-Wesley, 1986), pp. 187,
   192–193; American Academy of Allergy and
   Immunology, *An Allergic Reaction* (Milwaukee,
   WI: 1988); P. Janet, "Our Immune System: The
   Wars Within," *National Geographic* magazine,
   June 1986, pp. 702–734.
2. Material on the effects of histamine in certain areas
   of the body developed from Earl Ubell, "They're
   Wiping Out Allergies," *Parade* magazine, June
   1990, pp. 8–10.

## CHAPTER 2

Material on inheritance and statistics of allergies developed from Paula Dranov, *Allergies* (New York: Random House, 1990), pp. 4–7; Robert Feldman, M.D., and David Carroll, *The Complete Book of Children's Allergies* (New York: Warner Books, 1986), pp. 46–50; U.S. Department of Health and Human Services, *Asthma and Allergies: An Optimistic Future* (Washington, DC: 1980).

## CHAPTER 4

1. Materials on pollen developed from Stephen Lyons, "Weed!" *In Health*, May/June 1990, pp. 74–77; American Academy of Allergy and Immunology, *Understanding the Pollen and Mold Season* (Milwaukee, WI).
2. Materials on regional forecasting for hay fever developed from conversations with experts who develop the Chlor-Trimeton Allergy Season Index and from American Academy of Allergy and Immunology. *Hay Fever, Pollen and Molds: The Pollen Season* (Milwaukee, WI).
3. Materials on rise of hay fever in Arizona developed from Valerie Fahey, "Which Seasons Are Worst— Turn Your Home into an Allergy-Free Zone," *Hippocrates*, March/April, 1989, p. 96; M. Eric Gershwin, M.D., and Edwin L. Klingelhofer, Ph.D., *Conquering Your Child's Allergies* (Reading, MA: Addison-Wesley, 1989) p. 46.
4. Deborah Franklin, "A Nose for Allergies," *Hippocrates*, March/April, 1989, pp. 88–94.
5. Franklin, "A Nose for Allergies," p. 91.
6. Materials used to develop section on molds and

spores from U.S. Department of Health and Human Services, *Asthma and Allergies: An Optimistic Future* (Washington DC: 1980); Paula Dranov, *Allergies* (New York: Random House, 1990), pp. 25–28.

7. Materials used to develop section on dust mites developed from Jane Brody, "Dust Mite Control," *New York Times*, September 27, 1990; "Relationship of Dust Mites to Asthma, National Study 1965–84," *Chest Magazine*, 1987, p. 655.

8. Materials on animal dander from Robert Buderi, "Sneezing...Don't Forget to Wash the Cat," *Business Week*, September 1990; "Make Holidays a Breeze—Not a Wheeze," *New York Post*, November 1989; Gershwin and Klingelhofer, *Conquering Your Child's Allergies*, p. 48.

## CHAPTER 5 _____

1. Materials used to develop section on food allergies include Stuart Berger, M.D., "Serious Health Problems Related to Food Allergies," *New York Post*, October 1, 1990; D. S. Sobel and T. Ferguson, *The People's Book of Medical Tests* (New York: Summit Books, 1985).

2. Robert Burke citation developed through interviews with Mr. Burke and used with his permission.

3. Materials used to develop section on food additives include Robert Feldman, M.D., and David Carroll, *The Complete Book of Children's Allergies* (New York: Warner Books, 1986), p. 178; Janice Wickerstaff Joneja, Ph.D., and Leonard Bielory, M.D., *Understanding Allergy, Sensitivity and Immunity* (New Brunswick, NJ: Rutgers University Press, 1990), pp. 188–190.

## CHAPTER 6

1. Claude M. Frazier, M.D., *Insects and Allergy and What To Do About Them* (Emmaus, PA: Rodale Press, 1989), pp. 57–62.
2. Materials used to develop section on drug allergies include Paula Dranov, *Allergies* (New York: Random House, 1990), pp. 59–64; Robert Feldman, M.D., and David Carroll, *The Complete Book of Children's Allergies* (New York: Warner Books, 1986), p. 193; and Janice Wickerstaff Joneja, Ph.D., and Leonard Bielory, M.D., *Understanding Allergy, Sensitivity and Immunity* (New Brunswick, NJ: Rutgers University Press, 1990), pp. 154–156.

## CHAPTER 7

1. Lawrence K. Altman, "Vigilance Urged in the Treatment of Asthma," *New York Times*, February 6, 1990, p. 21.
2. Materials used to develop section on asthmatic reaction include Janice Wickerstaff Joneja, Ph.D., and Leonard Bielory, M.D., *Understanding Allergy, Sensitivity and Immunity* (New Brunswick, NJ: Rutgers University Press, 1990), pp. 149–150; Deborah Tkac, ed., *The Doctor's Book of Remedies* (Emmaus, PA: Rodale Press, 1990), pp. 27–33; E. B. Weiss and M. S. Segal, *Bronchial Asthma*, 2nd ed. (Boston: Little Brown, 1985).
3. Materials used to develop section on asthma tests, management of the disease, and medicines in use include Decker and Kaliner, *Understanding and Managing Asthma* (New York: Avon Books, 1988); American Academy of Asthma and Immunology, *Asthma* (Milwaukee, WI: 1989);

M. Eric Gershwin, M.D., and Edwin L. Klingelhofer, Ph.D., *Conquering Your Child's Allergies* (Reading, MA: Addison-Wesley, 1989), pp. 95–98.
4. Paula Dranov, *Allergies* (New York: Random House, 1990), pp. 42–48.

## CHAPTER 8

Materials used to develop chapter include American Academy of Allergy and Immunology, "Allergic Contact Dermatitis," *Asthma and Allergy Advocate*, Spring 1989, pp. 3–4; American Academy of Allergy and Immunology, *Hives: Tip #10*, (Milwaukee, WI: 1989): A. P. Kaplan, R. H. Buckley, and K. P. Mathews, "Allergic Skin Disorders," *Journal of the American Medical Association*, 20 (1987): 2900–2909; Donald Vickery, M.D., and James Fries, M.D., *Take Care of Yourself*, 3rd ed. (Reading, MA: Addison-Wesley, 1989), pp. 192–195, 210–213, 218–224.

## CHAPTER 9

1. American Academy of Allergy and Immunology, *Allergic and Nonallergic Rhinitis: Tip #16* (Milwaukee, WI: 1988).
2. A. Knight, *Asthma and Hay Fever: How to Relieve Wheezing and Sneezing* (London: Martin Dunitz, 1981).
3. "Hay Fever," *New York Times*, November 6, 1990, p. C23; E. Ubell, "Treating a Drippy Nose: Some Promising Tests," *New York Times*, September 11, 1990, pp. 9–10.
4. Paula Dranov, *Allergies* (New York: Random House, 1990), pp. 29–31; M. Eric Gershwin, M.D.

and Edwin L. Klingelhofer, Ph.D. *Conquering Your Child's Allergies* (Reading, MA: Addison-Wesley, 1989), pp. 106–108.

CHAPTER 10 ⎯⎯⎯⎯⎯⎯⎯⎯⎯⎯⎯⎯⎯

Materials used to develop this chapter include W. Bierman and D. Pearlman, eds., *Allergic Disease from Infancy to Adulthood*, 2nd ed. (Philadelphia, PA: W. B., Saunders, 1987); American Academy of Allergy and Immunology, "Eye Allergies," *Asthma and Allergy Advocate*, Spring 1990, pp. 3–4.

CHAPTER 11 ⎯⎯⎯⎯⎯⎯⎯⎯⎯⎯⎯⎯⎯

Sources include A. M. Weinstein, *The Complete Guide to Self-Management of Asthma and Allergies for Patients and their Families* (New York: Ballantine Books, 1988). Sources for materials on testing include Paula Dranov, *Allergies* (New York: Random House, 1990), pp. 84–96. Sources for materials on clinical ecology include Lisa Belkin, "Sufferers Find Haven from Chemical World," *New York Times*, December 2, 1990, pp. 1, 32; Robert Reinhold, "When Life Is Toxic," *New York Times Magazine*, September 16, 1990, pp. 50–70.

# Glossary

**Adrenalin.** See Epinephrine.

**Allergen.** A substance foreign to the body that may trigger an allergic reaction. See Antigen.

**Allergenic.** Able to cause an allergic reaction.

**Allergic rhinitis.** Commonly called hay fever or rose fever when seasonal, perennial allergic rhinitis when symptomatic all year round. Symptoms include sneezing, runny nose, itching eyes and/or nose.

**Allergy.** A reaction to substances in the environment such as dust, pollen, animal dander.

**Alveoli.** The small air sacs at the ends of the smallest air passageways, where the transfer of oxygen and carbon dioxide takes place.

**Anaphylaxis.** A severe generalized allergic reaction immediately or possibly hours after exposure to an allergen. Symptoms may include some or all of the following: sneezing, nasal discharge, shortness of breath, wheezing, hives, swelling of throat and larynx, drop in blood pressure, unconsciousness, or even death.

**Angioedema.** An allergic reaction characterized by swelling of the skin and the underlying tissues.

**Antibody.** A protein manufactured by plasma cells to respond to a foreign substance (antigen) in the body.

**Antigen.** A foreign substance that causes the production of antibodies in the body, which activate an immune response. See Antibody.

**Antihistamine.** A drug used to treat allergic symptoms by blocking the effects of histamines, which are produced during an allergic reaction.

**Asthma.** A physical condition affecting the airways. Symptoms usually include shortness of breath, tightening in the chest, coughing, and wheezing.

**Atopic dermatitis.** A type of eczema, characterized by dry skin and itchy rash, usually located on the cheeks, elbows, wrists, and backs of ears and knees. See Eczema.

**Basophil.** A type of white blood cell coated with IgE antibodies. When chemical mediators are released from the basophil, an allergic reaction begins.

**Bronchodilator drug.** A drug that causes the bronchial tubes to relax, used in the treatment of bronchial asthma, bronchitis, and sometimes emphysema.

**Challenge tests.** Administering a suspected allergen to determine if an allergy is present.

**Conjunctiva.** Outer membrane of the eye. It can be irritated or inflamed by a nasal allergy.

**Contact dermatitis.** A rash that appears after the skin is touched by irritants, such as chemicals, some plants, detergents, metals, fabrics.

**Corticosteroids.** Drugs used to treat the swelling and inflammation caused by an allergic reaction.

**Cromolyn sodium.** Drug used in the treatment of hay fever and asthma.

**Danders.** Dead layers of skin that flake off an animal and cause an allergic reaction.

**Decongestants.** Drugs in the form of sprays or drops

that are used to relieve symptoms of the common cold and some forms of rhinitis.

**Dust mites.** Microscopic insects that live indoors. Their excreta is the main allergen in dust.

**Eczema.** An extremely itchy, scaly, and dry rash that usually appears behind the ears and knees or on the cheeks, elbows, and wrists. See Atopic dermatitis.

**Elimination test.** A procedure that eliminates certain foods from a diet if it is suspected that those foods cause allergic reactions.

**Emphysema.** An irreversible lung disease that causes the destruction of the alveoli.

**Epinephrine.** A chemical produced in the adrenal gland that is used to treat asthma.

**Eustachian tube.** Located in the back of the throat, leading from the nose to each ear, these tubes balance the air pressure in the eardrum.

**Fungi.** Primitive organisms that are common allergens. See Molds.

**Generalized allergic reaction.** A severe reaction that may simultaneously affect the lungs, skin, nose and eyes, and heart. See Anaphylaxis.

**Hay fever.** Symptoms such as sneezing, runny nose, tearing, itchy eyes, congestion, fatigue and irritability that appear during the seasons of plant pollination; medically known as rhinitis.

**Histamine.** A chemical released by the mast cells during an allergic reaction that can cause the itching, runny nose, teary eyes, and other symptoms associated with hay fever.

**Hymenoptera.** Those insects (bees, wasps, hornets, yellow jackets) responsible for most allergic reactions to stings.

**Idiosyncrasy.** An abnormal response to a drug though no absolute allergic reaction can be found.

**IgE antibody.** An antibody responsible for producing an allergic reaction when it interacts with an antigen.

**Immune System.** The body's defense mechanism: organs, cells, and chemicals that protect the body against diseases.

**Immunotherapy.** Allergy treatment involving injections of small amounts of allergens. Also called allergy shots or desensitization.

**Lymphocyte.** A white blood cell that can produce antibodies that are important in the immune process.

**Mast cells.** The cells that are sensitized when an allergy is present, releasing histamine.

**Mediator.** A chemical compound that causes symptoms during an allergic reaction.

**Mucous membrane.** The lining of the mouth, throat, nose, and other body cavities.

**Mucus.** The fluid secreted by the mucous glands to protect and moisten the mucous membranes.

**Pollen.** A grain containing the male reproductive portion of trees, grasses, and weeds.

**Rhinitis.** A nasal condition characterized by sneezing, runny nose, congestion, itchy eyes. If the condition is present seasonally, it is usually hay or rose fever. If it continues throughout the year, it is known as perennial allergic rhinitis.

**Sensitized.** Exposure to an antigen that has caused the immune system to produce specific antibodies.

**Skin tests.** Also called intradermal, prick/puncture, or scratch tests. They are used to detect the presence of allergic IgE antibodies.

**Spirometer.** An instrument that measures obstruction in the airways.

**Spores.** The reproductive parts of a mold plant. These allergens float in the air and are abundant in the spring, summer, and fall.

**Theophylline.** Frequently prescribed bronchodilator for asthma treatment. See Bronchodilator drugs.

**Urticaria.** Hives.

**Wheeze.** The sound created by asthmatics who have

difficulty breathing because of the buildup of mucus in the airways and the narrowing of the breathing tubes.

**Xanthines.** Bronchodilating drugs for asthma treatment. See Bronchodilator drugs.

# For Further Reading

The Asthma and Allergy Foundation of America and Craig Norback, eds. *The Allergy Encyclopedia*. New York: NAL/Plume, 1981.

Berland, Theodore, and Lucia Fischer-Pap. *Living with Your Allergies and Asthma*. New York: St. Martin's Press, 1983.

Dees, Susan C. *Allergy*. Burlington, NC: Carolina Biological Supply Company, 1988.

Edelson, Edward. *Allergies*. New York: Chelsea House, 1989.

Mumbry, Keith, illus. *The Allergy Handbook*. New York: Sterling, 1989.

Silverstein, Alvin, and Virginia B. Silverstein. *Allergies*. New York: Harper and Row, 1977.

White, Tony. *Living with Allergies*. New York: Franklin Watts, 1990.

# Index

# About the Authors

Between them, Gerald Newman and Eleanor Newman Layfield have contributed eight books to Franklin Watts, some individually and some together.

Besides being an author, Mrs. Layfield is currently a management consultant to major communications companies and serves as an adjunct professor at the University of Colorado Business School.

Mr. Newman has written educational films, newspaper and magazine articles, and books on various subjects. He teaches writing to gifted students and is also a freelance graphic designer.